# The Making of the Museum of Scotland

## Charles McKean

NMS Publishing Limited

Published by
National Museums of Scotland Publishing Limited
Chambers Street
Edinburgh EH1 1JF

© NMS Publishing Limited 2000

Text: © Charles McKean

Cartoons on pages 31, 103, 110, 113-116 by Don Aldridge
Illustrations on pages xiv and xv by Jim Tate
Photography unless otherwise credited by
Neil Maclean and others in NMS Photography
Designed by Elizabeth Robertson of NMS Publishing Limited

**British Library Cataloguing in Publication Data**
A catalogue record of this book is available from the British Library.

ISBN 1 901663 11 6

# Contents

# Acknowledgements

Many are owed thanks for their assistance with this project – above all the ghost of Lord Bute, whose idea it was after the competition of 1991. Jenni Calder tirelessly provisioned it with files and guidance, and Sue Macgregor and Allen Simpson were indefatigable in tracking down, with the help of the NMS Library, unknown paperwork, files, documents, drawings and reports.

The curators and staff of the National Museums have been exceptionally helpful and candid. Thanks are due particularly to Mark Jones, Ian Hooper, Hugh Cheape, David Clarke, Alison Cromarty, David Caldwell, George Dalgleish, Dorothy Kidd, Mike Taylor, Rose Watban; and to Sheila Brock, Mary Bryden, Jim Tate and his staff, Mike Spearman and the multimedia unit, Griff Boyle, James Simpson, Russell Eggleton, Stephen Richards, Susan Mitchell, Elspeth Alexander and Flora Johnston. It was memorable to watch the Exhibitions Review Committee address the sample display case. In addition I would like to record my gratitude to Helen Kemp, Lesley Taylor and Elizabeth Robertson of NMS Publishing Limited for their help and guidance during the making of this book.

Discussions with the Earl of Perth, Sir Robert Smith, Sir Alistair Grant, Prof Peter Jones, Prof Tom Devine, Paul Clarke, Paul Devine, Ben Tindall, Mike Macaulay, Murray Grigor, Prof Chris Whatley, Colin Bell, Allen Simpson and John Spencely illuminated dusky corners. The Museum, the RIAS and Ben Tindall kindly allowed access to their files.

To Gordon Benson, gratitude for meetings in airport lounges, coffee houses and Piranesi-like building locations; and to all those in the Mildmay Grove *atelier* (particularly Eleanor), with its *fin-de-siècle* sun-dappled meeting room crammed with bits of models. Finally, thanks to Lena Smith for the transcription of notes, extracts and interviews; and to my family whom this book supplanted for too long.

Opposite:
The Museum of Scotland from the esplanade of Edinburgh Castle, with Arthur's Seat in the background.

# Introduction

National institutions often greet the completion of major developments with commemorative booklets, which illustrate the building and list the commissioning and design team, the dignitaries entertained and the order of service. This book is a substitute. It has its origins in a museum's *raison d'être* being to explain the context of its objects in order that they might be better understood. This volume is an attempt to do the same for the Museum of Scotland itself: namely to record the context of its creation so that it may be better understood.

It is about an idea that first emerged from a simple proposal to rename a museum collection, which germinated, developed, and finally bloomed as the competition-winning Museum of Scotland in Chambers Street, Edinburgh. It seeks to explain how the idea was transformed into a brief; why the brief contained what it did; the processes leading to commissioning the architect; and the judging of an architectural competition. It follows how the brief changed and how the building responded to it; what lay behind the devising of the displays; and, finally, how all these separate strands synthesised into a single building that may come to represent Scotland. The *idea* may be embodied in glowing tawny stonework, standing as a sentinel where Chambers Street debouches into medieval Edinburgh. There is, however, another museum – several forests-worth of sheer effort and over 24,000 drawings, files, notes, sketches and photographs that lie semi-dispersed in plan chests, filing cabinets, vaults and closets. Accumulating since before 1929, the paper museum itself merits a David Mach or George Wylie installation.

This book is not a guidebook to the Museum of Scotland. During most of its preparation, the spaces were still cavernous and darkened, Piranesi-like, obscured by scaffolding save where lit by swaying light bulbs, apertures sealed with barely translucent paper. It is, rather, about decision-making: government decisions, museum decisions and curator decisions that ultimately led to design decisions (and sometimes vice-versa). It has been excavated from the extraordinary quantities of discussions, seminars, meetings and papers preponderantly in the files of the former Royal Scottish Museum, the National Museums of Scotland and the Royal Incorporation of Architects in Scotland. Neither the whole story nor the only story, it may be characterised as the story that champions the building.

The building is inseparable from its time. It is the embodiment of ideas about Scotland and how to portray them which were first discussed over 200 years ago, and it surmounts and resolves decades of dispute. For most of the twentieth century,

> **" I am occupied in writing of our history, being assured to content few and to displease many therethrough. "**
>
> George Buchanan 1582, commenting on his then unpublished *Rerum Scoticarum Historia*

> **" The new Museum of Scotland is neither a title nor a building, but rather a concept to be developed. "**
>
> Marquess of Bute[1]

Opposite:
The Museum of Scotland's Hawthornden Court.
*Niall Hendrie*

The Museum of Scotland
from Forest Road.
*Charles McKean*

the land it occupies was the subject of a tussle between two competing, dissimilar and mutually suspicious museums – the Royal Scottish Museum (RSM) in Chambers Street and the National Museum of Antiquities of Scotland (NMAS) in Queen Street. Only in the late 1970s was it finally accepted that the restricted size of the site could not accommodate two separate organisations. With the government then in power, two sites were out of the question: ergo the two institutions had to merge. In summer 1983 the Secretary of State for Scotland announced that the two museums were to be joined in a single organisation, a marriage solemnised by the 1985 National Heritage (Scotland) Act. It is not often that a major public institution is created by the spatial limitations of a plot of ground.

Under the chairmanship of the sixth Marquess of Bute, the Trustees of the National Museums of Scotland emerged as patrons. Since his aspiration was to make the creation of the Museum of Scotland an act of distinction, the selection

The Hawthornden Court
looking west, with the
Dupplin Cross marking
the entrance to *The
Kingdom of the Scots*.

and appointment of the architect had to follow impeccable procedures; and the opportunity to design the building had to be open to all architects. The resulting architectural competition became improbably controversial. In the late 1980s, architectural competitions had become the thing of the moment, not least as the consequence of the Prince of Wales' dramatic attack on the shortlist for the competition for the National Gallery in Trafalgar Square in 1984, which had led to the process being abandoned. A further intervention into the competition for the rebuilding of the Paternoster Square area around St Paul's had followed. The flourishing competitions scene in Scotland had been exempt from such royal scrutiny – until the Prince accepted the role as President of the Patrons of the new museum.

Then there was the spectre of Scotland to be addressed. The title 'Museum of Scotland' had emerged in 1980, the same year that Barbara and Murray Grigor astounded Edinburgh with their examination of kitsch entitled 'Scotch Myths'. Its

climax was a pianola, against the background of a Scots panorama, foaming to the strains of Mendelssohn's 'Fingal's Cave'. To begin with, the 'Museum of Scotland' may have implied only the retitling and relocation of the existing collections of the NMAS, but expectations were soon inflated. People had aspirations for it – aspirations of national identity far beyond a mere collection of antiquities. When the competition-winning architects came to encapsulate such notions in a building, they had as an aim that it should be 'a benchmark for the quality of Scottish cultural endeavour at the end of the twentieth century'.[2] In their view at least, this was to be the building by which *fin-de-siècle* Scottish architecture was to be judged, no less than the National Monument on Calton Hill had been the benchmark for the Athens of the North.

The museum sought a new relationship between architecture and artefact. The extremes of museum design are museums as 'boxes' offering total display flexibility and museums as art galleries for the display of historic cultural objects. The box – 'white box' for art galleries and 'black box' for museums – signifies a space that offers curators maximum display freedom and flexibility with minimum architectonic interference. Architectural pyrotechnics are therefore limited to the façade and to the spaces outside the galleries: the entrance hall and principal circulation spaces.[3] By contrast, objects in the 'museum as art gallery' are carefully isolated, decontextualised and displayed as iconic art works – as, for example, in Sir Robert Smirke's British Museum, in the work of the Italian architect Carlo Scarpa, or in Barry Gasson's Burrell Collection, Glasgow, where the design is a primary contributor to the experience. Would the language of the design conflict with or dominate the objects? After all, architecture is intensely vocal. (When asked why he had wrapped the Reichstag in Berlin, the artist Christo replied: 'Because I wished to silence it.' He failed: instead he lent it a different language.) A sensitive architect, however, does not design a museum that overwhelms its objects.

The Museum of Scotland project set out to find a middle path between the art-object museum and the black-box museum. The completed building not only offers a narrative of Scottish history based upon surviving objects; it has also become an exhibit itself. Its design lends unprecedented significance to many of its contents.

Museums customarily collect and preserve collections, and are eager to share them with visitors and scholars. There is the excitement of the chance addition to the collection – something like the Cramond lioness, its stone hindquarters gently iron-stained, crunching an early person's head in the basement. The scope, surprise, condition and presentation of their collections reflect the expertise of the curator. That was the original context for the Museum of Scotland project; but it developed, instead, as a thematic museum intended to convey 'the story of a whole nation'.[4] Displays organised around chronologically-based narratives were not unprecedented, but what distinguished the Museum of Scotland was the scale. The intent being to present a national narrative while maintaining the depth of knowl-edge embodied in the collections, themes were both derived from – and supported by – the objects in the collections. This required curators, designers and visitors to make novel and occasionally surprising connections.

There were the architects' concepts and the curators' concepts. The displays themselves were the product of intensive market research, consultation and consumer testing. Each concept has been buffeted, tested and refined to achieve a synthesis. Yet it was not until everything was in place that the interrelationship between the displays and objects and the architectural intention became clear.

The Museum of Scotland, its displays and its architecture, will soon be taken for granted, as though it had always been there. Occasional questions might be asked: what took it so long, why does it look like that, and what was the fuss about? That is what this book hopes to illuminate.

## Notes

1  Bute to the introductory meeting of the Museums Advisory Board, 12 May 1984.
2  Interview with Gordon Benson.
3  See particularly I Bercedo, A Puyuelo and I Sen: *The architecture of museums*; and Victoria Newhouse: *Towards a New Museum*.
4  Interview with Mark Jones.

Excavations

Oct 93

Foundations

Jul 94

Gallery 22

July 96

Structure for the Bristo Port tower

Nov 96

The tower structure rises

June 96

A broch takes shape

Sept 96

July 96    Pouring the first floor

Sept 96    Upper storeys emerge

March 97    The Bristo Port tower

April 98    Steamboat architecture

July 97    Topping out the tower

May 98    The form emerges

# Grown from the rock

### Analysing the *genius loci*

Just an undistinguished grassy slope by the time of the international architectural competition in 1991, the site selected for the Museum of Scotland was potentially one of the most resonant in Scotland. Overlooked by the castle to the west and by Arthur's Seat to the east, and just visible from the Royal Mile, it was jostled by history and by historic monuments. Its latent power was enormous.

The design of the Museum of Scotland could have been approached solely in terms of extending, deferentially, the footprint of the Royal Scottish Museum (RSM) with a somewhat blank new building, as was to be proposed by the Property Services Agency in the late 1960s. Conversely, it could have been occupied by a more or less separate and self-referential architectural monument, as most entrants to the architectural competition were to suggest. However, a new building on that corner, when assessed against the qualities of the place within its wider urban context, also offered the opportunity of reconnecting eighteenth-century south-side Edinburgh with the mediaeval landscape of the Grassmarket and its closes, from which it had been severed by the intrusion of George IV Bridge in 1827. The intensity with which Benson + Forsyth identified with that underlying *genius loci*, and designed in response to it, was crucial to their selection as winner of the architectural competition.

### The beginnings

The lands on the sunny slopes south of old Edinburgh had originally been home to the clergy: the Blackfriars, the Greyfriars, and St Mary's in the Fields Collegiate Church (more notoriously the Kirk o' Field). After the Reformation, education was substituted for religion, and it was on former monastic lands that grew the University, the Grammar School, George Heriot's Hospital, Surgeons' Hall, the Trades Maidens Hospital and the Royal Infirmary – with the alcoholic leavening of a brewery in 1598 from which the site's ancient name 'Society' derived (see Competition note one, page 53). In the eighteenth century three adjacent but unrelated *soi-disant* squares – Adam, Argyle and Brown's – putatively 'after the London manner', filled some of the space left over.

Change to the south side became rapid after the completion of South Bridge in 1788. A fundamental shift in the city's axis took place – from east-west to north-south – underscored by the way that Robert Adam's rebuilding of the double-courtyard University, 1789-93, faced east to South Bridge, whereas its

> **" Remember. The building is there, but has not yet been uncovered. "**
>
> *Douglas Cardinal reporting the views of his tribal elders prior to designing Canada's Museum of Civilisation.*

Opposite:
The Museum of Scotland tower goes up on the site next to the Royal Museum.
*Niall Hendrie*

1

Looking up Advocate's
Close in Edinburgh's
Old Town towards the
High Street.
*Charles McKean*

Renaissance predecessor had faced north across the Cowgate. Construction of what is now called the Old College began with pomp and enthusiasm, but halted incomplete only a few years later, 'an immense ruin, a monument of vanity of which poverty has prevented the completion'.[1] It was eventually completed to a modified design by William Playfair between 1819 and 1827.

Thirty-four years later, 'the great and noble museum'[2] – what was to become the Royal Museum – erupted immediately west of the University across Horse Wynd to engulf Argyle Square and the Trades Maidens Hospital. The University was no longer able to finance, house or maintain its natural history collections adequately,[3] and it seized the opportunity to combine with the proposed Industrial Museum for Scotland, paid for (partly, at least) by the profits of the 1851 Great Exhibition. Founded in 1854, the new museum (popularly known as the Chambers Street Museum) was formed from the merging of Edinburgh University's Museum of Natural History with the Industrial Museum; and it was completed in 1864 as the Edinburgh Museum of Science and Art.[4] Since students and staff still needed access to its collections as teaching aids, the natural location was the unreformed Renaissance jumble abutting the University's west flank, and access between the two was provided over a bridge curving above West College Street. The new museum was designed in 1861 by Captain Francis Fowke of the Royal Engineers. To the street he presented a Venetian Renaissance palazzo representing learning and culture, behind which he concealed the structural gymnastics of the soaring iron, wood and glass exhibition halls representing the latest in applied industrial technology and prefabrication techniques. We should not be surprised at this Janus-faced design. A culture that had to apply frilly stockings to the legs of pianos would certainly take fright at unadorned iron columns. A Venetian doublet would do very well.

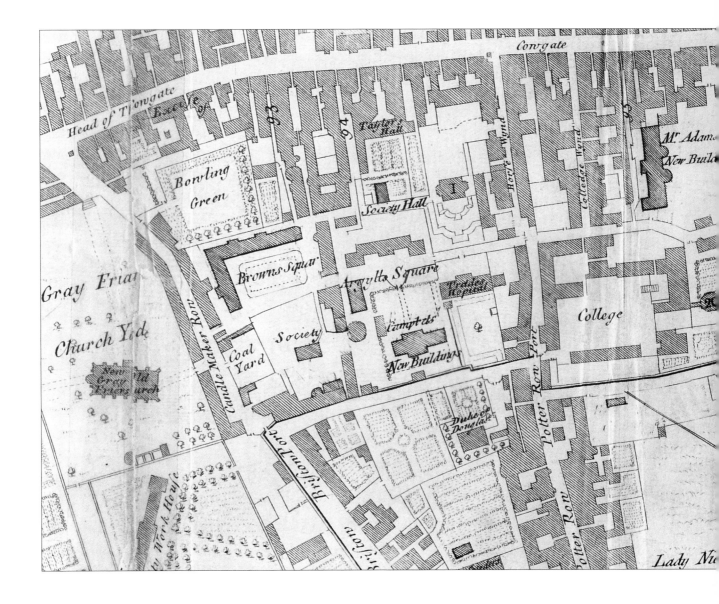

Thus did the south side of Chambers Street establish its monumental character even before the street was formed. Begun in 1867 under the City Improvement Act, and named after publisher Lord Provost William Chambers (chief promoter of city improvement), the new street was driven not by slum clearance, as had been behind the creation of Cockburn Street, St Mary's and Blackfriars Streets, but by a desire to cleanse the urban irrationalities of the past. It linked the new axes of Edinburgh – the two new bridges – and provided south Edinburgh with a new east-west communication to parallel both the High Street and George Street. Following the approximate line of North College Street, it cut across one of the primary ancient entrances to Edinburgh from the south (Potter Row Port and Horse Wynd – commemorated in West College Street), and swept away the remaining squares.

Detail from a map by William Edgar, 1742, showing Brown's Square and Society, the site of the Museum of Scotland. The Royal Museum occupies the site of 'Argyll' Square.

The new street, paved in 1876 with wooden blocks at a cost of £6000,[5] was too short and wide to be a street, and too narrow, attenuated, and insufficiently orthogonal to be a square. It displeased the stern men of the Architectural Institute of Scotland (AIS) who recommended that it should be 130 feet wide and left open right down to the Cowgate, adorned with fragments of Renaissance Edinburgh that would have become available if their deranged plan to rebuild the entire Old Town had matured. The museum could thus have been gazing out over an early heritage sculpture park.[6] Mercifully, the AIS plan went unrealised, and worthy institutions began to cluster – beginning with the Watt Institution and School of Arts. Precursor of Heriot-Watt University, it relocated from Adam Square to a building erected in 1872-3 from designs by David Rhind. Now the Crown Office, the building is lucky still to be there. In 1971, Heriot-Watt had enthusiastically contemplated dismantling its façade and re-erecting it at the new campus in Riccarton.[7] Then followed a Church of Scotland Training College, a church, the Phrenological Society's Museum, a surgical hospital and a Dental School. The Victorians were proud of their imposing street 'edificed into four large blocks, three or four storeys high, in ornate examples of the Italian style, with some specimens of the French'.[8] It had become a stumpy and somewhat dreary educational boulevard.

Chambers Street lacked architectural focus and urban design quality. It was neither straight nor level. Its street walls were not parallel, and its roofscapes varied

from an austere Adam cornice to a frivolous openwork cast-iron dome. Within their generally four-storeyed scale the façades were collectively incoherent. The street sloped eastwards to gaze downhill upon the undistinguished South Bridge, the louche end of neo-classical Edinburgh, or upwards to the west, into the void created when George IV Bridge was cut through medieval Edinburgh in 1827-34. The sole levity was provided by a Theatre of Varieties on the corner of South Bridge. The south-western end of the street, still called Society, remained largely untouched and dormant: some ancient relics, the George IV Hotel, pubs, a Heriot Trust school[9] and a Chinese restaurant were all demolished in 1973 in preparation for a new museum due imminently on site.

It remained a grassy slope for the next twenty years and never received the landscaping or the monumental industrial sculpture planned for it.[10] It seemed natural, indeed logical, that the site should be used for an extension to the Royal Scottish Museum, as Sir Frank Mears had suggested back in 1929. But there was another contender.

Chambers Street – 'a somewhat dreary educational boulevard' – with the Edinburgh Museum of Science and Art (now the Royal Museum) on the right. Watercolour of around 1870 by David Cousin and Sam Bough.

Joseph Anderson and George Black in the National Museum of Antiquities whilst located at the Royal Institution (now the Royal Scottish Academy) in 1890. Some of the NMAS's most treasured possessions, including the Stirling Heads, are on display.

## A marriage of convenience

The National Museum of Antiquities of Scotland had been born as the museum of the Society of Antiquaries of Scotland, founded as an act of national assertion on 14 November 1780 by the earnest but eccentric peer, David Steuart Erskine, 11th Earl of Buchan (possible original of Walter Scott's antiquary Jonathan Oldbuck). Buchan's intention was to prevent more antiquities and 'monuments of ancient greatness' leaving Scotland for the south.[11] Enough, after all, had already left in 'Byng's schyppes' from Fraserburgh after the Jacobite rising of 1745.[12] He wrote to Robert Barclay of Urie in 1784: 'I consider the elucidation of the first dawn of History in my Country as no mean or frivolous employment adapted to the plodding Antiquary only, but to the Historian and the Patriot.'[13] In his introductory discourse, he had conjectured: 'The most unpopular studies … become interesting and useful to all, and are pleasing even to the fluttering sons and daughters of dissipation. I do not expect that we shall be able to introduce antiquities with the *Morning Post* at breakfast …. But a great point would be gained, if they could be rendered interesting amusement for a long winter night'; thereby confirming Archibald Constable's observation that when he chose to be intelligible, no one was more distinguished for the talent of ready wit. Buchan managed to persuade John Stuart, third Earl of Bute, to be the Society's first President.

When Buchan was buried in 1829 he was laid with his head to the east instead of to the west. At the graveside Henry Cockburn heard Sir Walter Scott murmur: 'Just let him lie since he is there. Odd bless ye, I knew the worthy Earl all my life, and I never knew his head right in my days.'[14]

The Society of Antiquaries' first significant collection was an astonishing pile of Bronze Age weapons, then thought to be Roman, dredged from Duddingston Loch. It obtained a royal charter, and

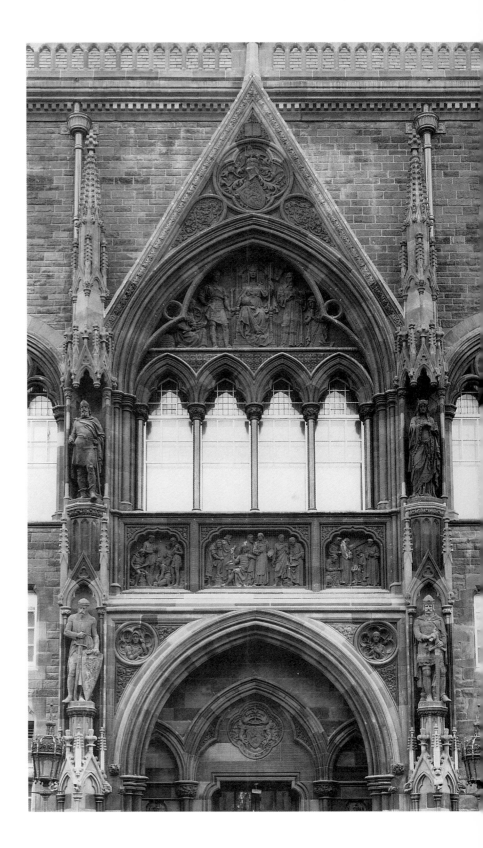

soon built up a collection of valuable coins, medals, portraits, manuscripts and objects of antiquarian interest. Its members helped create the widespread perception of the antiquary at large: a 'paradoxical figure: brilliant but bigoted, convivial but cantankerous, scholarly but simple, at once astute and credulous and eccentric and conventional, witty and wise and dull and plodding by turns'.[15] After quitting its original building in the Cowgate, however, the Society led a peripatetic life of sharing premises, first with the Royal Institution from 1826, and then with the Royal Society of Edinburgh (RSE) in George Street from 1844. In 1851 it made its collections over to the State in return for premises, staff, the first call on all Scottish Treasure Trove, and a fitting-out grant. Yet over the next forty years there were still attempts to move the Antiquaries or to change their status, implying government unease with their location within Scottish society. In 1868 there was a plan to merge them with the Museum of Science and Art, in 1875 with the RSE, and in 1882 a further plan to relocate them into the upper storeys of the museum's west wing (which they rejected unless they were offered the entire wing).[16] In the meantime their collection had swollen from 2000 objects to 70,000, mainly through gifts from Fellows or from excavations, enhanced by a few purchases made with their lilliputian Treasury grant of £200.

In 1884 the proprietor of *The Scotsman*, John Ritchie Findlay, proposed to gift a new building, sharing only a central entrance, for the National Portrait Gallery and the Antiquaries whose collections he thought 'mutually illustrative'.[17] Designed by Robert Rowand Anderson in Queen Street, its west wing was occupied by the Portrait Gallery in 1889 and the east by the National Museum of Antiquities of Scotland in August 1891. The Keeper was unenthusiastic about the building's suitability. To Anderson's statement that he considered the medieval French architecture appropriate, the Keeper is alleged to have replied: 'You should therefore have turned the windows upside down.'[18]

In 1929 came the first formal statement that the museum should move: the time was 'not so far distant when the Museum of Antiquities will require a separate building if it is to play the part it ought to play as an educational institution':[19] and the following year the Antiquaries' Council favoured a site near Brown's Square[20] on the other side of Chambers Street to the present building, thus first directing their attention to that part of the capital. Ten years later they were still hunting the necessary 'generous donor'[21] for that site. Twenty more years and a World War later, nothing had transpired, and the Standing Commission on Museums and Galleries demanded government action. It was unimpressed by the museum's organisation or condition. The Society of Antiquaries ran the building, but its Keeper was a civil servant, occupying a public building that provided accommodation for a private society. Since the museum had moved to Queen Street, attendance had fallen from 100,000 per annum to barely 30,000. Since – in bureaucratic terms – the museum was a mess, it should be reconstituted as a national institution.[22]

A leisurely two years later therefore, in April 1951, the government appointed Sheriff J R Philip to produce a report.[23] Finding displays 'lamentably cramped' with no room for expansion, he recommended that the museum move elsewhere, perhaps associated with a Scottish National Folk Museum,[24] but not into a large suburban house like Kelvingrove: 'We are unanimously of the opinion that a central site is to be preferred somewhere in the triangle of the Royal Scottish Museum, the University and Princes Street – preferably near the Royal Mile.' The new building should be worthy of a national institution, but Philip warned that 'certain types of architecture, however aesthetically pleasing, do not suit the functions of this type of museum'.[25] This latter incantation was almost certainly directed at the 1951 South Bank exhibition with its Skylon and its dangerously innovative buildings of glass and new materials.

In 1953 the government approved the purchase of the site west of the Chambers Street Museum, implicitly accepting the Philip Report. On 1 April 1954, the National Museum of Antiquities of Scotland was constituted as 'the national repository for Scottish artifacts other than pictures' with its own Board of Trustees of 21 members.[26] The timing implied – to the NMAS Trustees at least – that the site had been bought for them.[27] To the NMAS staff, the report and its subsequent Act of Parliament promised a new building and 'a new deal',[28] and it sent their advisers to scout the site. 'After ascertaining that the Royal Scottish Museum (RSM) was not interested', it was agreed that the site still suited the NMAS very well. However, whoever had done that 'ascertaining' with the RSM must have used Nelson's telescope, and seen only what he wished to see. For Mears' 1929 suggestion in *The Scotsman* that the remaining Society site should be used for an extension to the RSM had reflected the RSM's own perception of being grossly short of space. It had no intention of relinquishing its expectations for the site next door.[29] Progress

continued languidly for the remainder of the decade and – so far as the government was concerned – the urgency implied in the Philip Report seeped away. NMAS Trustees were kept warm by annual progress reports that implied (but did not evidence) action. The Ministry of Works had taken only 'preliminary steps toward acquisition' by 1957.

Once it was purchased, however, the total site available for museum expansion was very much larger than that now occupied by the Museum of Scotland. It extended further into George IV Bridge and a long way south, crossing the current Lothian Street to Bristo Square. The government had been amassing land to the south and west of the RSM since World War I, and in the 1950s had built the RSM lecture theatre, with a cafe in its foyer, on its eastern edge as the first phase of truly grandiloquent expansion plans. The purchase of the west Chambers Street site was regarded by the RSM as the final, necessary piece of the jigsaw to allow it to occupy the entire city block. Unedifyingly, the government appears to have promised two different museums the same plot of ground. So civil servants cheerfully dreamt up a compromise: why could they not share it between them?

With seeming Scottish Office approval, the RSM's then Director, Dr Douglas Allan, reiterated in 1961 'our needs are such that we shall eventually need the entire site';[30] and only acquiesced to contemplate how it might be shared under pressure, and then solely on the condition that the RSM retained the Chambers Street portion, which he preferred, relegating the Antiquities to the Lothian Street site; and even then subject to the Property Services Agency architects confirming that the space was adequate. How much better, he wrote, if the Portrait Gallery could be

The RSM with the site on which both it and the NMAS hoped to build. The 'southern site' stretched from the buildings on the right south to Lothian Street and east to where the RSM's lecture theatre is – about twice as large again.

The National Museum of Antiquities crammed into Queen Street.

moved from its building (which it owned) to the Royal High School (which would have to be purchased), thus releasing the entire Queen Street building with its Gothic windows for the NMAS. Six months later, his position had hardened: 'It is not a good thing that any part [of that site] should be shared by the NMAS. I would strongly deprecate sharing the site with any other Institution .... The RSM is four museums in one, all expanding .... A really special exhibition hall is going to be needed .... So is a restaurant .... Some day, there should be a planetarium.'[31]

Ten years after the Philip Report, the government had nothing to show for it. It spent the next two years increasing pressure on the RSM to share the favoured Chambers Street corner with the NMAS (who were certainly not going to be fobbed off with a site facing the tundra to the south). As a diversionary tactic, Allen touted other sites for the NMAS – particularly favouring a location alongside the Royal College of Surgeons. Unfortunately, the University's campus development plan proposed by Percy Johnson Marshall included a south-side multi-level bypass to replace Nicolson Street (perspectives of which are held by the University). The site was due to disappear. Allan remained obdurate: 'I emphatically oppose sharing a site barely adequate for our ultimate expansion.' Although sympathising with the congested conditions of the NMAS, he suggested 'that the importance to the public of a major expansion of our scientific and technological collections would far outweigh a new deployment of the collection of Scottish antiquities'.[32] So the museums were moving closer toward a position of mutual despite,[33] and with no clear champion the site boundaries began to contract. As the city undertook partial implementation of the University's grandiose campus plan, over 23,000 square feet of the southern site were sliced off by the re-alignment of Lothian Street.[34]

The Scottish Office increased the pressure on the museums to come to an accommodation. There was

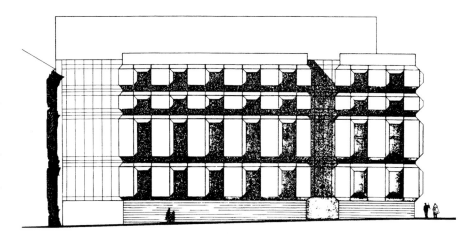

no pretence that it was for operational efficiency – for it implied a substantial reduction in ambition for both bodies. It was the simple consequence of the government's developing eye for parsimony. The Standing Commission on Museums and Galleries' agreement on the condition that 'the plan for a joint building was officially accepted as temporary'[35] set the tone for the next ten years: sharing the site was merely an expedient measure designed to assist the museums with an immediate problem. Eventually the NMAS would move out to something purpose-designed, leaving the RSM as end-user.

But when it came to design, the virtual impossibility of this bureaucratic nostrum – even in the interim – soon became apparent. The 'prestige hall' the NMAS naturally desired, within a building that expressed the NMAS identity, was incompatible with a long-term use representing the identity of the RSM. Furthermore, the latter's new Director, Ian Finlay, had his heart set on a planetarium on top, which might prove an uneasy companion for a baronial hall beneath. Both museums required specifically crafted spaces for themes or objects which would cause problems once either institution moved out – as each wanted the other to do. The alternative – a featureless, characterless, yet flexible building, designed for joint use by two very different museums for only about twenty-five years, and one that could not be customised to reflect their identity – was not what NMAS Trustees thought they had earned by waiting patiently over the previous fourteen years. The Ministry of Public Buildings and Works (MoPBW) architects Robert Saddler and Trevor Mann proposed designing two separate buildings within one shell, each with a certain level of customisation.[36] That bred a new set of difficulties. Would the NMAS have its own entrance? Was the split to be vertical or horizontal? To what extent could support staff and services be shared? Was there even to be a link between the two museums and – if so – who would hold the key? (The Standing Commission

The shape of museums to come: two schemes that never happened:
1) The Mann scheme of 1971
2) The Revised scheme of 1972.

remarked irritably that that was something that surely the two museums could organize.[37]) Misery and angst characterised meeting after meeting.

In 1967 Ian Finlay obtained support for his beloved planetarium from Professor Hermann Brück, Astronomer Royal for Scotland,[38] and the following year Saddler went on a study tour to report on the best way of building one.[39] Clearly impressed by planetaria in Nagoya and Athens, he proposed adding a similar domed structure to the top of the western gable of the proposed building. Error. It now filled the periscope of the Royal Fine Art Commission for Scotland (RFACS). For while the Commission had been relaxed about change to the streetscape – and had indeed counselled the architect to 'experiment with a wide variety of materials, perhaps even brass or copper'[40] – it was paranoid about parapets. Condemning the planetarium as too bulky, it advised relocating it to the ground level for easier public access.[41] Fatal suggestion. The ground floor of the Chambers Street site was now the unassailable preserve of the NMAS, for whom twentieth-century planetaria were a low priority. (A Callanish upon the rooftop – as the later competition-winning design implied – might have been a different matter.) To Finlay's deep distress, the planetarium, for which he had fought for over ten years, was in danger of decapitation: 'So far as the Royal Scottish Museum is concerned, [a planetarium] was to be the feature which gave the new building meaning.'[42] Worn down by the continued non-appearance of the new building, and by the perpetual pressure to cede to the demands of the NMAS, he considered it no longer worthwhile to attend Joint Steering Committee meetings. If the planetarium were lost there would be almost nothing of benefit to the RSM being offered within the new building. By contrast, the NMAS Director, Dr Robert Stevenson, had had to forfeit only a single floor of his cherished ambition, and had, after all, won his mediaeval hall.[43]

That, at least, was the official story. Privily, however, Finlay had turned his attention back to the southern end of the site.[44] As far back as 1963 the RSM considered enfolding its entire western gable – from the new lecture theatre round into Chambers Street – with an enormous new construction, and Finlay commissioned a development study of the southern edge from the PSA architect Trevor Mann. Mann proposed a long four-storeyed building extending from the lecture theatre virtually to Bristo Place,[45] with a two-storeyed appendix surmounted by the dome of a planetarium. Scheduled for construction in 1980-4, the extension was to provide 5464 m² of exhibition space, offices, laboratories and workshops. It was Finlay's swansong.

In January 1972 Finlay's successor, Dr Norman Tebble, attended his first meeting of the Joint Steering Committee. A man prone to instant decisions and wholly committed to the RSM, he was given neither to pacifying civil service mandarins nor to opting out of committees. He read files and realised with dismay that the RSM had been left with only the top floor of the proposed Chambers Street building, reached only by a lift or a narrow spiral stair, with no loading or entrance facilities. He told the meeting: 'I reject the plan for the New Museum. Let us start again.'[46] The abandonment of the planetarium was 'an intellectual murder'.[47] (Intellectual genocide would have made little difference. Space problems and height problems had removed the planetarium.) Stevenson swatted Tebble's outburst briskly with a masterly rewriting of history: 'If the planning was to stop now, my staff would resign en bloc.' That the RSM had been given as much as the top floor in the building was a kindness, 'not as a result of traditional right'. Indeed, it was the first time that he had heard the planning of the new building being questioned.[48] The files indicate otherwise.

Privately, proposals for the southern site were continued, but Mann's development update report of June 1972 indicated new – and more urgent – priorities. Tebble had discovered that his building of architectural distinction was no longer capable of meeting contemporary museum standards,[49] and there was even a plague of mice visiting from Lothian Street. The first step was the installation of adequate environmental controls and air conditioning. So proud was Tebble of his new strategy described in the Triennial Report in 1973[50] that he had it symbolised by the graphic design on the front cover. The tiled floor of the Main Hall was replaced by travertine, and there was almost complete internal reconstruction in the north-west and north-east wings – the Evolution Exhibition in the latter being opened by the Duke of Edinburgh in 1975. Departments began a lengthy period of such jockeying for space that curators invented a game on the lines of Monopoly called 'RSM', the winning department having succeeded in taking over the entire building.[51] The southern extension and its planetarium, with minor design alterations, remained central to the strategy, but was pushed back in the programme to 1984-6.

The RSM was an integral part of the Scottish Education Department (SED) and the latter did not permit Tebble the luxury of withdrawing from the

The main hall of the Royal Museum, showing the travertine marble floor which replaced the Victorian tiles in 1971.

13

joint project on Chambers Street. Never ceasing to attack the fundamentals of the project, he nonetheless allocated his floor to a Gallery of the History of Science, and permitted his staff to collaborate as necessary with colleagues in the NMAS. As the architects attempted to modify design after design to satisfy the two museological gladiators, the site was further tightened by the widening of Lindsay Street, and the plans were perpetually subject to the sleepless eye of the RFACS scanning the horizon for intruders. Hoping to persuade the Scottish Education Department of the project's folly, Tebble informed it that the project was 'the wrong building in the wrong place', emphasising that agreement by the Standing Commission for Museums and Galleries had been conditional upon receiving Treasury Ministry assurance that sharing by two museums would be *a temporary arrangement only*.[52] Now, however, the proposed building was to be so carefully customised for the NMAS that it could never successfully transfer back to the RSM. He lamented directly to his employer, the Secretary of State, that the RSM was weakened because it had no Trustees[53] and had to rely on civil servants instead.

Target dates for construction, originally set for 1967, had been extended to 1969, then 1970. Demolition of the existing buildings, planned for 1971, was postponed to 1972. Tenders were again due by August 1973, October 1973, and then again delayed until the end of 1974. Tebble then tried again. He produced a new assessment of the space requirements of the RSM that demonstrated, unsurprisingly, that their share of the new building was virtually irrelevant to the RSM's real needs, and sought a complete review of the project.[54] Further deadlines went by as it became clear that it was impossible to satisfy two separate institutions' accommodation on that tight site.

Just months before a final, agonisingly agreed scheme was actually due to start on site, the project expired, with many others, when the Prime Minister announced the 'party was over' in early autumn 1976. The forthcoming referendum on Scottish devolution appears to have had no impact whatsoever, for the project remained dead. Unsubstantiated rumour had it that some of the money thereby released was used to fund the Burrell Gallery in Glasgow.

In March 1978, Tebble and Mann revisited their Museum Development plan.[55] The focus moved internally with a plan to convert some of the galleries into 'multi-floor study collection areas'. For environmental control and fire safety, the original top-lit galleried wells of Halls 10, 11, 12 and 22 were unsatisfactory, causing 'so much frustration both to keepers and to display staff' and should be floored out. Not only was the west site in limbo, but problems had now emerged to the south. In the fond belief that Andrew Baird's Scientific Laboratory and shop had in fact been that of John Logie Baird, the buildings framing the entrance to Brighton Street had been listed as being of architectural and historic importance. It was no longer possible to conceive of a single building lining the southern boundary.

Cartoon by Ian Lyster, 1976, greeting the recent installation of a new air conditioning system.

## Rethink

In February 1979 Dr (later Sir) Alwyn Williams was invited to chair a Committee to enquire into the scope of functions of the national museums in Scotland. Thirty-five years had passed since the Philip Report with nothing to show for it but disillusion, and the Committee encountered widespread demoralisation resulting from 'the understandable belief that little was worth doing because of an impending move that never came'.[56] It met fourteen times, visited all existing national museums and galleries in Scotland and fourteen local ones, and took oral and written evidence from over 100 individuals and organisations.[57] To assist in its discussions the RSM issued a questionnaire to visitors, and from the underwhelming 153 responses it learnt of a public demand for an improved restaurant, better interpretative booklets, and later opening hours.[58] Evidence from partisan groups largely rehearsed old arguments. The Friends of the RSM regarded it as of 'the highest

importance to the Museum being able to grow on and beside the site it now occupies', whereas the Museums Association attacked the conditions in Queen Street as 'grossly inadequate'.[59]

The Williams Committee was terminally unimpressed by the succession of abortive schemes for the Chambers Street site, 1964-76, dismissing them as 'wasteful and misdirected'.[60] It bent its mind most toward the NMAS. 'It has been the curation and display of things Scottish which have been most neglected in the past.' The NMAS collections should be retitled the 'Museum of Scotland' and housed in 'a showplace for Scottish culture'.[61] Providentially, the Trustees of John Watson's School, across Belford Bridge, had just decided to put their great neo-classical building and its eleven acres onto the market, and the Crown Estates Commissioners had bought it for public use. The Commissioners had come into a windfall from the charges paid by oil companies to lay pipes across

The Newcomen engine as an urban art installation. 1970s proposal by the PSA for the interim use of the Museum of Scotland site.

the foreshore, and the Earl of Perth had convinced his fellow Commissioners that the money should be spent in Scotland.[62] All museums were invited to express an interest. The NMAS Trustees and staff, however, remained aloof: it would be a poor exchange for their inadequate premises in Queen Street, unsuitable in form – 'our showcases would not fit' – and it was far too far from the centre. The National Galleries, however, attracted by its wide corridors protected from direct light, swiftly accepted it as the new home for the Scottish National Gallery of Modern Art which had long outgrown its delightful eighteenth-century villa, Inverleith House, in the middle of the Royal Botanic Gardens.[63]

On 15 August 1980, the Williams Committee took the unusual step of dissenting very publicly from the NMAS by publishing an urgent interim recommendation to the Secretary of State.[64] It strongly advocated the establishment of the proposed new Museum of Scotland in John Watson's School – provided it was enlarged by some 60% to the rear, to a total of 9810 m². The Modern Art Gallery would be much more comfortable in the vacated space in Queen Street, rubbing shoulders with its cousin, the Portrait Gallery. Lord Perth, in the meanwhile, tried to persuade the NMAS Trustees to change their mind. It appears that they did,[65] but the National Galleries, having grasped such a prize, would not relinquish it, and so the Modern Art Gallery it became.

Williams' final report recommended the establishment of a Scottish Museums Commission, possibly to prevent a repetition of the internecine troubles of the previous decades, and favoured travelling exhibitions and loans to local museums. It enthused about education. It recommended a Museum of Lowland Life, possibly in association with the National Trust for

Scotland.[66] There should be a Museum of Industry, preferably in Glasgow's Queen's Dock, utilising the substantial industrial collections of the RSM.[67] The RSM should be permitted the Chambers Street site to itself. The only major proposal it rejected was a separate Museum of Religion, ironically now realised by the City of Glasgow in the St Mungo Museum beside Glasgow Cathedral.

The Committee had also supported Dr Tebble and his RSM staff who, in those tremulous years of the first Thatcher quinquennium and market-testing, opposed the plan to make the RSM a trustee museum (despite the fact that only eight years previously he had petitioned the Secretary of State to the effect that he had felt vulnerable to the NMAS because he *lacked* Trustees), since they desperately wished to remain civil servants. Williams concluded: 'It is efficient, well run, and the staff wish to remain in the Civil Service.' It appears that the Committee believed that most problems could be solved by granting everybody (save the clerics) what they sought. It was perhaps over-optimistic to have anticipated that government largesse might increase accordingly in those days of emerging slump.

The Williams Report, published in 1981, attracted unprecedented attention to the condition of Scotland's museums, and highlighted their unexplored educational function and potential. That something had to be done was now on the political agenda. In July 1982, the Secretary of State, expressing gratitude to Dr Williams and his team, proceeded to dismember the report, with the notable exception of the proposed Museum of Scotland. He rebuffed both the idea of a Scottish Museums Commission[68] and continuing civil service status for the RSM. The RSM was to be transferred to a board of Trustees, on the grounds that it deserved 'greater independence from Government, more in keeping with its international reputation'.[69] A consultative paper issued in August on whether there should be a single board for a unitary organisation for both museums, listed far more reasons in favour (administration, efficiency and use of resources – support services, planning, overlap, and effective accommodation) of a single board of Trustees than against. To the two institutions feeling threatened, the suggestion that their prestige might increase as a result of merger lacked conviction.

Consultation proved acrimonious. There was mutual concern about loss of identity. NMAS staff having business with Tebble were prone to being harangued. Since they had rejected the Williams Committee's proposal to move to John Watson's as being entirely inappropriate, they regarded the government's decision to merge the two organisations as revenge.[70] Tebble titled the relevant file the 'Hiving-Off File'. In a furious letter to the Scottish Education Department in October 1982, he excoriated the very notion of a joint museum: 'The Royal Scottish Museum is being asked to compare two organisations, one – itself – which exists, and the other, the proposed Museum of Scotland, which does not exist.'[71] Whilst RSM staff wished to remain civil servants, some NMAS staff were resentful about their lower grading, and particularly feared the loss of their specialist identity. Condemning 'transitory politicians and temporary committees', Tebble considered it futile to respond to the consultation paper as it stood. Radical MPs were recruited: Robin Cook pledged to oppose. In vain.

## Nuptials

The Secretary of State, George Younger, had dithered until he had considered Sir Max Rayner's report on the Victoria and Albert and the Science Museums: and then decided to do something similar in Scotland. On 6 December 1983 he informed Parliament that the right course was to have a single board served by one director. On 16 April 1984, the post was advertised. The following day the Marquess of Bute was appointed Chairman of a new Museums Advisory Board with the task of achieving a single museum organisation. But before the first meeting of his Board could be convened, the Department of the Environment in London, charged with realising surplus government assets, achieved their entire annual target for Scotland by selling off the southern site, seemingly without enquiring of the Scottish Education Department whether there were any proposals for its use. In a graceful letter to Tebble, possibly covering what might have been a Cabinet row, Angus Mitchell of the SED wrote: 'Ministers took the view that the Chambers Street site was sufficient.'[72]

Thus it appeared that the ideas of both museums, which had, at one time, expanded to require the equivalent of John Watson's School expanded by two-thirds, and the Chambers Street site, and the 4500 m² offered by the southern site, were all to be condensed, and shrunk into an appendage at the western end of the Royal Scottish Museum.

## Notes

1 James Stark: *A Picture of Edinburgh*, p 437.
2 James Grant: *Old and New Edinburgh*, vol II, p 274.
3 Charles D Waterston: *Collections in Context*, p 81.
4 R B K Stevenson: 'The Museum, its beginnings and its development' in A S Bell (ed): *The Scottish Antiquarian Tradition*, p 144.
5 Grant: op cit, p 274.
6 Minutes of the Architectural Institute of Scotland, 1858-61.
7 Royal Scottish Museum: Steering Committee file 1.6.0, 1961 ff, minutes 23.3.1970.
8 Grant: op cit, p 274.
9 Used, until the 1930s, as the Watt Institution's Library.
10 PSA drawing 2, August 1976.
11 Iain Gordon Brown: *The Hobbyhorsical Antiquary*, p 6.
12 David Fraser (ed): *The Christian Watt Papers*, p 9.
13 Brown: op cit, p 45.
14 Ibid.
15 Ibid, p 46.
16 Stevenson: op cit, p 156.
17 Ibid, p 170.
18 Ibid, p 173. It quickly outgrew its new space, which, in any case, was not particularly well suited to the museum's needs – 'oppressive red brick walls' having to be painted cream in 1948.
19 Ibid, p 193. The 1929 Royal Commission on the National Museums and Galleries in London and Edinburgh.
20 Ibid, p 194.
21 R B K Stevenson: 'The National Museum of Antiquities of Scotland – a review' (Edinburgh, May 1972). Also New Building Working Group Minutes 26.1.1987, paper 4: 'History of the New Museum Building', taken from the files of NMAS Trustees by A Kennedy, July 1972.
22 Third Report of the Standing Committee on Museums and Art Galleries, 1949.
23 The Philip Report. The Philip Report correctly states the date of the move to the Queen Street building as 1891 (14 August), two years before the *Buildings of Scotland: Edinburgh* (Edinburgh 1984) claims the building was complete.
24 Ibid, para 16.
25 Ibid, paras 33 and 38. The report defined the museum's potential audience in the following order of priority: professional historians and archaeologists; university students and postgraduates; Fellows of the Society of Antiquaries; Schools and Workers Educational Institutes; and – lastly – the ordinary sightseer and enquirer (para 31).
26 1954 National Museum of Antiquities Act: clause 14.
27 The NMAS charter also extended its responsibilities to embrace Country Life, which led eventually to establishing the Scottish Agricultural Museum at Ingliston.
28 Stevenson: 'The Museum, its beginnings and its developments', p 200.
29 New Building Working Group Minutes 26.1.1987, paper 4: 'History of the New Museum Building'. On 8 February 1929, Sir Frank Mears had written in the *The Scotsman*: 'The Royal Scottish Museum and the Royal Infirmary are looking to great extensions.' There is no evidence that it had relinquished the ambition: indeed, to the contrary.
30 Dr Douglas Allan, Director RSM, 22.6.1961, in file 1.6.0 (RSM

Steering Committee file). He recommended that the Portrait Gallery be relocated to the soon-to-be-abandoned Royal High School on Calton Hill, so that the NMAS could have the entire building on Queen Street, and cease its predatory proposals for Chambers Street. This is repeated in a letter to W V Wastie, MoPBW, 22.9.1961. Allan's successor, Ian Finlay, identified the Department of Technology as 'especially starved' (30.7.1964).

31 Raised by Dr Allan 18.9.1961.

32 Letter by Dr Allan to the Scottish Home and Health Department 6.4.1964; also New Building Working Group minutes 26.1.87, paper 4: 'History of the New Museum Building.' The 10th Report to Trustees of the NMAS stated: 'It would not be possible for us to share a building indefinitely with another museum'; whereas the 12th Report contains details of a feasibility study for a very large site for both museums, of which the NMAS was intending to enjoy *circa* 37,000 m², of which 19,000 m² was display. The RSM was to receive just 10,000 m², and they were to share 11,000 m² of common services.

33 10th Report to Trustees of the NMAS.

34 Steering Committee Minutes 20.5.1966. See also, the University of Edinburgh Comprehensive Development Plan 1963. Its plans show an enormous building redevelopment wrapping its way around the western end of the RSM. An undated report, probably 1964, possibly produced for the Standing Commission on Museums and Buildings, emphasises that the site was clearly too small to accommodate both museums for more than a comparatively short period (file 1.6.0). When the Royal Fine Art Commission for Scotland came to consider the design six years later, it was informed: 'This building was a purely temporary expedient to relieve congestion within the museum' (RFACS Document 642: 23.02.1970).

35 Miss A L T Oppé, Secretary to the Standing Commission, to R B K Stevenson 6.10.1964. However, both museums were to agree on a 'prestige building which would make a major contribution to the architecture of Edinburgh': Minutes of the Steering Committee 5.6.1966.

36 Brief issued 20.5.1966. Steering Committee file.

37 Letter from Mrs Granger-Taylor of the Standing Commission to SED 21.8.1972. Royal Scottish Museum: Steering Committee file 1.6.0, 1961 ff.

38 Steering Committee file, 1967. In August 1968 the Treasury voted £1.5 million for the planetarium. Finlay's justification was that since the RSM was going to get very little additional useful space, the museum needed 'something really significant to draw in visitor numbers' (memo to SED, 7.7.1969). He warned the SED that the planetarium was 'a must', and that he would sacrifice space for it.

39 Robert Saddler 'Planetaria'.

40 RFACS Document 596. Minutes 27.01.1969.

41 Ibid. Also Steering Committee Minutes 16.11.1971. The RFACS had demanded, elegantly, that 'certain impedimenta on the roof should be lowered out of sight' (Finlay to SED, 18.1.1971).

42 Ian Finlay to MoPBW 14.3.1970. Steering Committee miscellaneous papers.

43 Steering Committee Minutes 14.5.1973.

44 For no mention appears in the Joint Committee Minutes.

45 Trevor Mann: 'Royal Scottish Museum future development Feasibility Study'.

46 Steering Committee Minutes 4.5.1972. Tebble had a point. In design development, the NMAS had gained 4000 ft² and the RSM had lost 10,152 ft².

47 Ibid 25.1.1972.

48 Tebble's handwritten notes of the meeting held on 25.1.1972. Stevenson had conveniently forgotten his undertaking to Ian Finlay of 13.4.1964: 'The NMAS would never wish to cling on to the Chambers Street corner in rivalry to RSM claims on it.'

49 Information from Dr Allen Simpson: confirmed in the second Mann report.

50 Royal Scottish Museum 'Triennial Report', December 1973.

51 Information from Dr Allen Simpson.

52 Quoted in Tebble's enraged resume of the entire saga to I M Robertson of the SED, 16.3.72. The Williams Report, appendix IV, 'Interim report to the Secretary of State for Scotland' and the addendum (p 89) contains much more detail on the matter of the Crown Estates Commissioners, John Watson's and the Gallery of Modern Art.

53 Steering Committee 4.5.1972.

54 Ibid 13.5.1972.

55 Trevor Mann: 'Royal Scottish Museum future development Feasibility Study Mark 3'.

56 Williams Report, para 2.6.

57 Ibid, preface p ix.

58 RSM News 7.2.1980, file 3.7.2 (Williams Committee miscellaneous papers).

59 Ibid, Report to Williams Committee 15.11.1979.

60 Williams Report, para 4.18.

61 File 3.7.2, Report by the Friends to the Williams Committee, para 4.

62 Interview with Lord Perth.

63 Interview with Lord Perth.

64 Williams Report, addendum, p 89.

65 Williams Report, appendix IV, para 13.

66 The Museum of Scottish Country Life, to be run jointly by the NMS and NTS, is under construction 18 years later at Wester Kittochside near East Kilbride.

67 Some of which were later loaned to Summerlee Industrial and Irvine Maritime Museums.

68 Albeit adding a Commissioner for Scotland to the Museums and Galleries Commission.

69 *Hansard* 22.7.1982.

70 Interview with Dr David Caldwell.

71 Contained within a memorandum to Joint Trustees 26.10.1982.

72 On 9 November 1983 the Secretary of the Scottish Education Department, Angus Mitchell, informed Tebble of the impending sale of the land and buildings to the south.

# A fresh start

The selection of Lord Bute for what could have been the ticklish task of marrying two institutions of fundamentally different character and tradition was accidentally masterly (he had not been the Establishment's first choice). Although both museums had enjoyed a decade of relative prosperity, enthusiastically acquiring staff and objects, the abortive museum project had created severe inter-institutional strain. Myths about each other had grown up to the point of caricature. Some NMAS staff, inclined to regard themselves as scholars and gentlemen, could be snooty about their RSM colleagues, viewing the RSM in the light of a Workers' Educational Association. Conversely, RSM staff prided themselves on being subject specialists in contrast to the period generalists over at the Antiquaries. To counteract such fissile tendencies, senior staff from both museums combined to issue a public letter enthusiastic about the potential of merger, welcoming the new organisation, and eagerly anticipating early collaborative projects.[1]

John Bute brought enormous sensibility, charm and lack of starch. A private person who abhorred public disagreement and squabbling, he would take soundings from as many people as he thought expedient, and make each person believe they were his trusty confidante. The files reveal just how many individuals caught up in the complicated machinations behind the Museum of Scotland felt privileged in the belief that they had been Bute's sole consultee. His eyebrow-raising postcards from foreign lands, adorned with a precisely scripted one-line quip or quiddity, were collected by their recipients. Thus was his network strengthened. Above all, he was unthreatenable and unbribable. Official displeasure or the withdrawal of favours held no terrors for him. When crossed, as he was many times during the gestation of the Museum of Scotland, Bute addressed ministers and their civil servants forcibly and bluntly (albeit sheathed in the most silken strophes) in a way risked by few others.

The relevant attribute, so far as the Scottish Office was concerned, may have been Bute's role as a notable patron and descendant of notable patrons. Sedulously attempting the completion of the interior of his ancestral seat, Mount Stuart on the Isle of Bute, with carvers, painters and gilders, he was a vigorous patron of Bute Fabrics (Rothesay), the Dovecote (tapestry) Studios (Edinburgh), and of Ben Dawson Furniture (Musselburgh). He was also a patron of the 1984 Festival of Architecture in Scotland. At his shoulder stood Nigel Pittman, who had quit responsibility for museums and galleries at the Scottish Education Department

> **" He was a bold man who first swallowed an oyster. "**
>
> Attributed to James VI

> **" By means of patience, common sense and time, impossibility becomes possibility. "**
>
> General Sir Colin Campbell

Opposite:
Looking through to the Royal Museum from the east end of the Hawthornden Court.
*Niall Hendrie*

21

John Crichton-Stuart, Sixth Marquess of Bute, continuing a lineage of patronage from his grandfather and great-grandfather. Chairman of the Trustees of the National Museums of Scotland, 1986-93.

(SED) to become Secretary to the Trustees. Pittman combined a formidable knowledge of inner government workings, which he bent to the benefit of the museum project, with an engaging and soothing manner.

Keen to make all those participating in the new adventure share his standards and ambitions, Bute opened the first meeting of the Museums Advisory Board (MAB)[2] by informing its members of his style: business would be conducted informally and by consensus; and not infrequently, with a great good humour.[3] Robert Smith, latterly Chairman of NMS Trustees, recalled the rare camaraderie of the MAB, whose members so enjoyed their task and each other's company that they held reunions thereafter. (When four of them were summarily removed as Museum Trustees in 1988, 'it felt like genocide'.[4]) The task was enormous. NMS outstations were studied and guidance sought on substantive staff issues, duplication of activity, information storage and retrieval, administration, and multiple libraries. The breadth of the Board's scrutiny emerges from its discussion papers: *A Museum of Industry for Scotland* by Dr Neil Cossons, Director of the Science Museum (accepted as framework); *The National Museum of Wales* (useful); *Museum Automation* by Professor Sidney Michaelson, then adviser to the NMS Research Laboratories (not relevant at this stage); *What and who should museums be for?* by Sir Kenneth Alexander (accepted); *Research* by Professor Andrew Walls (noted); and *Title of the Museum* by Lord Bute (no view taken). Although the Group's starting point had been the Williams Committee report, it did not feel necessarily bound by its conclusions.

The urgent need for a fully integrated museum structure became apparent from the Board's very first visits. The National Museums of Scotland had twenty-one sites – museums, outstations and storage facilities – predominantly in Edinburgh and neighbourhood, but also at locations in Dumfriesshire, Greenock, Biggar and the Lothians.[5] Condition was variable, and management *ad hoc*. 'We observed that there were many ways in which the Museums were failing to live up to their potential. Major collections were not on display or were displayed inadequately, without sufficient contextual materials to interest the visiting public …. Many of the reserve collections were housed in wholly unsatisfactory accommodation, to the potential danger of the items they contained. This represents a serious neglect and under-use of a major part of the cultural material heritage of Scotland.'[6] Displays failed to come up to standard in significant areas of both museums and there was a significant lack of twentieth-century visual arts material.[7] The Board concurred with Williams' emphasis upon presentation, education and communication – 'a major purpose of our national museums must be to enlighten, instruct and stimulate' – but cautioned lest populism be at the expense of scholarship.[8]

A new organisation certainly required a new broom. Norman Tebble retired as Director of the RSM, and the then Director of the NMAS, Dr Alexander Fenton, took the role of Research Director. In August, Dr Robert Anderson, who had been

Assistant Keeper 1970-5, returned from the Science Museum to become the National Museums of Scotland's first Director. He immediately sought out his colleagues' aspirations. Expansively, the heads of department replied that they would fain increase their permanent display facilities by some 300%, from a gross of 13,272 to 39,102 m²,[9] which Anderson duly fed into the discussions. Tainted by realism, the Board opted for a target two-thirds less – namely 8500 m². Storage space was in even greater crisis as a consequence of expansionist collecting policies. It was already 75% short, likely to reach 100% short within a decade.[10] Since there was no sense in investing any more money in the unsuitable Findlay Building in Queen Street, priority should be given to the redisplay of the existing NMAS collections in order to develop a coherent display of material illuminating Scottish history and culture – in a new building.[11]

The proposal for a Museum of Industry in Queen's Dock, Glasgow, aroused almost as much public interest and discussion as that for the setting up of a Museum of Scotland,[12] particularly once the Scottish Development Agency offered support for a mini-synoptic Museum of Industry within the Scottish Exhibition Centre.[13] The Board duly took off to study the National Maritime Museum, Greenwich, the Ironbridge Gorge Museum, and the Industrial and Maritime Museum in Cardiff Docks. Impressed as they occasionally were, Dr Cossons' view that Scotland's industrial history was 'inextricably bound up with other aspects of Scottish culture and life over the past two centuries and more' proved more persuasive. It made no sense 'to divorce industry in its widest sense from the other themes which will have to be brought out in the displays which will be developed on Scottish history and culture'.[14] Scottish industry would be integrated with the other aspects of Scottish development within the Museum of Scotland itself; and the notion of a separate National Museum of Industry in the west of Scotland expired. The strategy for Scotland's industrial development should be to encourage a 'network of devolved elements based on the *in situ* preservation of industrial sites and on a number of theme museums'.[15] Several industrial museums accordingly opened *in situ*, including the Scottish Mining Museum and Heritage Park, Lady Victoria Colliery, Newtongrange, and Summerlee (Coatbridge).

The integration of industrial objects with prehistoric flints was another demonstration of how the new Museum of Scotland would contain significant material from both museums rather than solely derived from the former NMAS collections. In the Board's view, only the greatest possible degree of integration of the two collections would realise the Williams Committee's concept of a Museum of Scotland 'most realistically'. The concept they adopted was to organise displays around 'two recognisable strands of activity: one focusing on the history and culture of Scotland, based very largely on the existing working collections of the NMAS; and one reflecting international themes and aspirations and drawn in large parts from the existing collections

Dr Robert Anderson (right), Director of the National Museums of Scotland 1984-91, with Malcolm Rifkind, Secretary of State for Scotland, who announced government support for the Museum of Scotland in 1989.

The model of the Bell Rock lighthouse featured in this late Victorian depiction of the RSM's displays. It is one of many objects contributed by the RSM to the Museum of Scotland.

and work of the RSM'. This clever compromise none-theless implied that these two existing collections could, between them, furnish a comprehensive national museum. Only during display development could that assumption be tested adequately.

## Which site?

The Civil Service had emphasised that ministers had determined to limit their largesse to the Chambers Street site and no further, so the Board decided to test that by considering a number of other locations[16] – but it was not in a position to undertake a full option appraisal for alternative sites. It was best informed about Chambers Street, and an equivalent degree of investigation or appraisal for the other sites was impossible. So it was undertaking not so much a new site study as checking that the ministers' – and their own – stated preference for Chambers Street would not prove a grievous locational error.

Even had Trevor Mann's plan to floor in the RSM's galleries (and thus destroy one of its greatest qualities – that of light with volume) been completed, the old museum would have remained inadequate. Alternative buildings in Waterloo Place proved too expensive and

inflexible. The Dean Orphanage (now the Paolozzi Gallery) and Donaldson's Hospital were not 'directly on the normal Edinburgh tourist trail'; Donaldson's was too small in any case; but worst of all, both buildings were 'of considerable distinction' (bureaucrat-speak for being listed as of historic importance). Conversion for specific museum use would therefore be especially difficult and costly[17] and neither was sufficiently close to the mother site in Chambers Street. Only the Scottish & Newcastle Breweries' Distribution Depot in Holyrood Road[18] was a real contender. It emerged as by far the cheapest location, well able to accommo-date a museum development of 17,000 m² 'which would meet the requirements very adequately'.[19] The Board's fundamental priority, that all the principal facilities of the museums should be grouped on one site, 'could only be achieved in Holyrood Road at the adjacent brewery site (between Holyrood Road and the Canongate), but also required the plant and the buildings on the site to be demolished and a new complex of buildings constructed'. But a move to Holyrood would require the unthinkable – namely the abandonment of what the Board regarded as 'the best asset in terms of buildings at the museum's disposal' – Fowke's wondrous galleried building in Chambers Street.[20]

Curiously, this single-site logic did not automati-cally commend itself to the SED, for Anderson was required, at even a very late date, to justify why a site split between Chambers Street and either Donaldson's Hospital or a restored Linlithgow Palace (the pre-ferred option) would not work more efficiently and more cost effectively since the construction cost was – they thought – likely to be cheaper. Acquiescence to a single site development based at Chambers Street was clinched by a National Museums of Scotland (NMS) study which revealed that the number of likely visitors would halve if the Museum of Scotland were located in the periphery of the city, and halve again if any-where else in the Central Belt.[21]

24

There was some relief that the 14,000 m² that a five-storeyed building covering almost the entire west Chambers Street site could provide was 'not out of line with what the museum will require in the near future'. The Board clung to the idea of more space being extracted from the site, but since it had also given priority to respecting the height of the RSM, and leaving the unspectacular and heterogeneous roofline of Chambers Street undisturbed, the only option left for the new Museum of Scotland was to burrow underground.

The principal recommendation of the MAB therefore was that a 'substantial new building' be constructed in close proximity to the Royal Museum. Significantly, 'no attempt should be made to provide a separate public entrance to it which might tend to detract from the sense of the museum's unity'.[22] Moreover, not only was the Museum of Scotland to be a mere extension to the existing Royal Museum, sharing the same entrance and staff, but it was going to have to include non-Scots material. For if a building on that truncated site were as far as government largesse was going to extend, and if it were to be the only building with the expected environmental conditions, then it would also have to house any other displays that required such conditions. As the brief developed, the building was therefore to contain two specialist galleries – one for Chinese lacquer and the other for ethnographic collections,[23] a united library from both previous museums, and an information centre.

The Board's final report contained a rocket directed at an ignorant, asset-stripping government. 'Our only regret is that the chance to provide for the possibility of yet further grouping of National Museums facilities around this common site has now been lost because of the decision taken very shortly before we began our study to dispose of the properties which back on to the present RSM building in Brighton Street and Lothian Street, which have been held in Crown ownership for nearly 80 years against just this eventuality. This was a misguided and short-sighted decision.'[24] Reports to government rarely criticise civil servants quite so caustically. It was a gauge of the extent of Bute's anger at the site's firesale.

On arrival, Anderson had found the Royal Museum building much deteriorated – 'in a shocking condition, with dry rot throughout'[25] – and relations with the Property Services Agency were problematic. They were accustomed to treat the building as their own, and the Director might arrive to find a gallery closed for works of which he had not been forewarned. Nor were the encounters of his staff with the Procrustean tendencies of the PSA's specialist museums' design unit always fruitful.[26] Thus, throughout the period of planning the new building, not only were alterations, improvements and repairs to the existing building continuous, but relationships with building professionals could be fragile.

On 27 February 1985 the Earl of Perth, a flamboyant supporter of the concept of the Museum of Scotland, added a clause to the Heritage Bill to the effect that the Board of Trustees of the new museum should have 'special regard to all matters

Scaffolding in the Royal Museum's Main Hall. The programme of building repairs and gallery refurbishment continued (sometimes unexpectedly) as the Museum of Scotland developed.

concerned with Scotland'; and that there should be permanent access for Fellows of the Society of Antiquaries of Scotland to their library in the new building. He was also to press for a guaranteed place for a Fellow on the Board of Trustees.[27] In October 1985 the Bill was enacted and Lord Bute became first Chairman of the Trustees of the National Museums of Scotland, his Trustees being the MAB members. The following year, he invited Robert Smith, who had been advising on the finances, to become his deputy. There was a celebratory party in the museum's Main Hall, and the Secretary of State's (slightly reluctant) attendance was greeted with blasts from a brass band on the balconies.[28]

Since the government's acceptance of his report implied acceptance of the need to build a new Museum of Scotland, Bute wrote to Malcolm Rifkind, new Secretary of State, seeking a meeting to discuss its funding. He received a Thatcherite response. Since Rifkind felt unable to commit funds to cover the cost of a major new building, a meeting would be inappropriate. He brusquely exhorted the Trustees to look to private sponsorship before any commitment in principle would be forthcoming from the government. The Trustees were displeased.[29] They had not been appointed to act as fundraisers so that the government could sidestep its obligations.

Bute decided to call Rifkind's bluff. What he required was evidence of how the collections could be used to communicate ideas about Scotland, a brief for the building, details of planning of the displays, and a prospectus. The latter would provide the basis of an appeal to the wider community. The Museum of Scotland would, this time, definitely emerge. Requiring 'a splash'[30] to maintain a high public profile, the NMS staged 'The Enterprising Scot' during the 1986 Edinburgh Festival, the first of a series of public exhibitions. (Subsequent ones were 'Scotland Creates' and 'The Wealth of a Nation'.) They were intended to contribute to the emerging museum brief, to test how the collections might be displayed, but – above all – to create public support for the new building in the teeth of government obduracy. 'The Enterprising Scot' was planned as a response to the 'Treasures of the Smithsonian' exhibition, to demonstrate the strength of Scottish culture and to travel internationally. Staged 'to investigate a new style of exhibition,'[31] it was held at relatively short notice and the selected location – the Royal Scottish Academy – was adverse. It required a new and costly power supply, and its services were inadequate. Although very well attended, the exhibition received mixed notices. It appeared to be conveying ideas that could not always be supported by adequate objects. The Camp Coffee advertisement used for publicity proved politically inappropriate for America, and Anderson later admitted that perhaps the Gerald Scarfe cartoon had been a mistake.[32] The exhibition did not travel. Worse, it had failed either to achieve significant collaboration between the staffs of the two museums or adequately to combine the collections. Perhaps it had underestimated just how slow cultural integration between the two museums was likely to be. It was an experiment, and 'the tensions that emerged taught us things that were valuable in the future museum'.[33]

With the exhibition out of the way, the NMS pressed on with its strategy of outwitting the government. In November, Trustee Ronnie Cramond[34] was asked to chair the ingloriously titled 'New Building Working Group'. Bute carefully crafted its role. It was to 'express the philosophy underlying the new building which will influence its form and which will animate what it contains'.[35] The crucial objective that the building's form should 'animate' the objects within was the clearest possible expression of Bute's determination that a 'black box' building would not be acceptable. The working group was also expected to define the new museum's functions, and its relationship with the existing Royal Museum building. Finally, it was required to create a demand for the new building by devising ways 'to persuade the people of Scotland that the new building, and what it could do, was something they absolutely must have'.[36] Cramond was brisk and proposed to keep meetings brief, business-like and infrequent.[37] His report 'The Proposed Museum of Scotland' was born nine months later.

His team chewed over the ideal attributes of the new building. Curatorial departments were invited to provide an outline of how their displays might ideally be structured and organised. The invitation, offered without limit of space, set imaginations soaring. (Inevitably, if the space finally available for display proved to be less, the process of exhibition development ran the risk of being perceived negatively.) They were also requested to make an initial selection of the most important primary objects or icons. (One suggested 'the waterwheel is a prime exhibit – if it is working'. The 1826 twenty-foot diameter waterwheel had powered an Aberdonian paper mill, and when set in Hall G 20, revolving daily at set times, it had been very impressive. But by 1987 it was growing old: its wood had begun to rot, and it had gone slightly off-balance. Although there was doubt whether it could be available in good condition, it survived into the competition brief and indeed onto the competition-winning drawings.)

As each department bid for space or facilities, there was much toing and froing. 'We are constantly asked for picnic space.'[38] There should be a tea room or restaurant on the top floor offering an exciting roofscape view of Edinburgh, areas for small receptions, and a shop. The report finally concluded that 14,000 m² could be extracted from the west end of Chambers Street – 8500 m² allocated to Scottish displays, 500 m² to two (250 m²) galleries of sensitive material, a combined library, a shop, restaurant, and office accommodation.[39] An Information Centre for Scottish Culture, located beside the library, was intended to enlarge the horizons and functions of the NMS by making it an active force for communication in the cultural life of Scotland – particularly for other organisations and institutions with relevant collections. Based on the NMS computer system, it would require a thirty-seat theatre or viewing area.

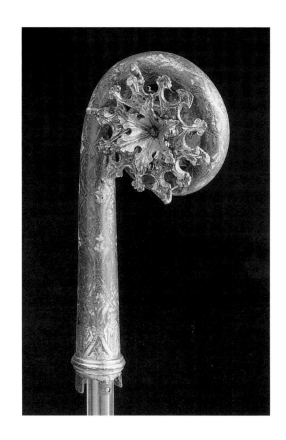

A late 12th-century crozier found at Whithorn Priory, one of the key exhibits featured in the initial curatorial lists.

27

An immediate question was to whom to turn for advice on building matters. The museums had hitherto been tied to the Property Services Agency, whose predecessors – the Ministry of Public Buildings and Works, and the Department of the Environment – had designed the abortive projects in the 1960s and 1970s. However, as part of the deconstruction of traditional patterns in the early 1980s, hived-off former government organisations – now Non Departmental Public Bodies – received compensatory freedoms, one of which was the liberty to choose independent design services. There was a lingering predisposition in the NMS to continue using the PSA, but its performance a decade earlier had been characterised neither by urgency nor by commitment. For instance, when requested by the Royal Fine Art Commission in 1974 to redesign the scheme to allow a view of the west pavilion of the Royal Scottish Museum, the PSA had responded that such a redesign would take eighteen months, and that 'it might be several years before the building could be reinstated in the programme'.[40]

The PSA architects' presentation to the Museums Advisory Board in December 1984, on 'how it worked now that the Crown Suppliers were on a fully commercial basis'[41] had been unimpressive, so the Board regarded itself thereafter as free to choose its architects as it willed. After a further meeting with the PSA, the Cramond Group – remaining lukewarm – sought advice from the Royal Incorporation of Architects in Scotland (RIAS) which recommended the selection of architect by competition. On 9 March 1987 – despite Trustee preference for an architectural competition limited to Scottish architects – the Cramond Group opted for selecting an architect by an open international competition.[42] Perhaps it had been influenced by the RIAS's somewhat messianic belief that since an international competition would attract worldwide attention it would help both to fundraise and to pressurise a recalcitrant government. For when the Secretary of State had finally found time to visit the Royal Museum, reiterating the rubric about private sector investment, Robert Smith – possibly incautiously – had suggested that private funds might be sought for the fitting out. The gleeful alacrity with which Rifkind grasped the offer upset Bute deeply. He considered the new museum to be a proper charge on the public purse, and that the government should be allowed no leeway. There was also the suspicion that if private sector funds were not forthcoming, the government might use it as an excuse to abandon the project altogether.

With the £20,000 obtained from the government to pay for a promotional prospectus, Cramond and Bute began one of those peculiarly British pavanes whereby the government refuses to spend a large sum of money but offers a small one that is then deployed against it. Reiver Associates from Galashiels was commissioned to write and design a brochure, which began long on words and short on illustration – and emerged the opposite. Entitled 'St. Andrew – will he ever see the light?', the brochure had a frontispiece of holograph signatures of all fifteen

Trustees. It was illustrated by photographs of warehouses full of dust-covered objects contrasted with photographs of the objects themselves. 'Let us lift a corner of those store-room dust-sheets and glimpse a few of the nation's many treasures; from fossils to flintlocks, pikestaffs to pomanders.' There was some deft rhetoric: 'We owe it to ourselves, our ancestors and our children to provide a lasting display of the cultural heritage of this small but influential nation. Scotland stands alone amongst countries of its size in having nowhere to tell the full story of its peoples and to show properly its many treasured possessions.' Then followed the curiously flaccid, 'This is a disgrace, long recognised by many'. It was a rather wet way of implying that the government had not yet recognised what was obvious. It closed with an exhortation: 'Don't test the patience of a Saint .... No ifs, no buts or maybes. No procrastination .... No more neglect or we will become the victim of our own inertia. That, in a nation which has provided some of the world's foremost innovators and explorers, would be unpardonable.' The brochures were dispatched to certain key marks in Scots society, as well as being widely distributed elsewhere, and recipients were invited to write to Bute to express their support, preferably accompanied by money. A 'fighting fund' of £17,000 emerged from the response. Ironically, St Andrew had had no difficulty in seeing the light. He had been on display, but nobody had checked. He was swiftly concealed.[43]

Bute would have been entitled to a wry smile as he genially dispatched a progress report to the Secretary of State on 3 July 1987.[44] A brief for the building was in draft, a patrons' committee was planned, a campaign director would be appointed for fundraising, and a buildings committee would be appointed the following year to plan the architectural aspects of the new building. Almost as a postscript, Bute drew attention to the St Andrew brochure he enclosed. It was the retaliation of the NMS Trustees to the Secretary of State's refusal to meet its chairman the previous year. They had utilised government money to produce a document implicitly attacking the government for prevarication, which appealed directly to the electorate over its head. Bute thanked Rifkind graciously for paying for it.[45]

## Feasibility

The outline proposals depended, to a large degree, upon PSA information, some of which might have become out of date. In 1988 architect John Richards (a member of the Williams Committee) was asked to undertake a feasibility study. He consulted with planners and architects, and studied contemporary museums. Protesting the extent to which his designs were notional and should not be taken as directions for any future architect, he had more or less to design the building to test the feasibility. His design was altogether rational: a nine-bay by nine-bay pavilion on five levels (including two mezzanines) capped by a fat, shallow-pitched roof, plant around the

St. Andrew

will he ever
see the light?

The cover of the brochure
published by the Trustees
to promote support and
raise a 'fighting fund' for
the new museum.

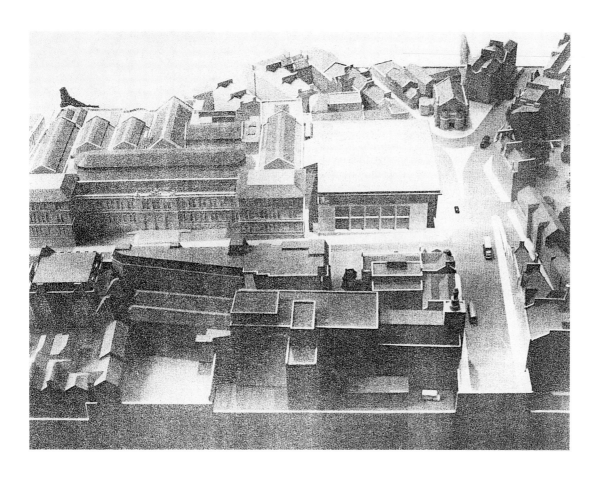

The scheme outlined in the feasibility study by John Richards, 1989.

perimeter, and rooflights glowing down upon the main circulation. Main banks of straight stairs lead up through the 'core' galleries at the centre, with study galleries to the edges. Critically, Richards concluded that although the museum could be accommodated on the site, approximately within cost, and according to the then developing brief, display space would be restricted to 6950 m$^2$.

The previous museum schemes had, under Crown Exemption, been exempt from planning permission. That no longer being the case, Richards went to negotiate. As always, the planners had stressed that they desired the very highest quality architectural design and choice of materials, and their phrase 'worthy of the building's important location' implied a stone-clad façade such as they had been requiring for solid areas of façade for years previously on sites of this importance. Under Richards' influence, they softened and said they would no longer object to other forms of cladding that might lighten the overwhelmingly dark character of the street – such as high-quality metal panels – and some generous areas of glass.[46]

The idiosyncratic character of Chambers Street had reached a totemic level, for Richards concluded 'the vacant site offers an opportunity to complete the south elevation of Chambers Street with a building which balances in quality and in its massing the flank wall of the University of Edinburgh's Old Quad. A new building on this site would form a link in a chain of buildings of international significance: the Old Quad, the Royal Museum of Scotland and, beyond the low buildings on Lindsay Place, Greyfriars Church'. Robert Adam's flanks were acquiring a status that he would never have accorded them in their original narrow confines of old North College Street; and if balance with the university had really mattered, the new building should have faced west onto Lindsay Place as the university faces east, leaving only the Royal Museum facing south. But, for traffic engineering reasons, planners would only contemplate the possibility of a secondary public entrance for pedestrians onto George IV Bridge. Moreover, they desired a gap between the new museum and the existing to replicate that between the RSM and the university. They trusted that account would be taken of views along Forrest Road and that the building envelope would 'be no higher than the tiled roof of the neighbouring building'[47] without seeing the need to justify such a restriction. Once again opportunities for exploiting the site were to be throttled by history.

### The emergence of the story of Scotland

Unconvinced by proposals to structure the displays according to theme, the Cramond Group proposed a chronological narrative. To keepers and curators accustomed to presenting and interpreting collections, chronology was not wholly welcome. David Clarke, Keeper of Archaeology, wrote 'the archaeological viewpoint is that approaches which use chronology as the basic structure are unhelpful to the effective presentation of archaeological collections', and preferred a thematic structure based upon subjects like power, processing, going out, coming in, and dialogues with gods.[48] He intended to group material for the 'Early Populations of Scotland' so that people could walk 'along' any individual theme seeing its development through time, or 'across' the five themes

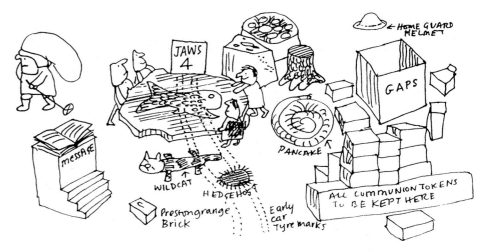

Cartoon by Don Aldridge commenting on Museum of Scotland aspirations.

or pathways that show the situation in a variety of human activities at given points in the past.

Elsewhere, the Cramond preference for a linear narrative was followed in the apportionment of the displays into sections: 'Making the Landscape', 'Kingdom', and 'Modern Scotland'. Collections of the archaeology of the Western Isles, the medieval church, the Scottish firearms industry, Scottish silver (form and function), Scottish glass (drink and decorum), the music of pipe and fiddle, and sport, were to be studied in greater depth in study galleries. 'Making the Landscape' would depict 'the striking correlation between Scotland's spectacular scenery and the underlying rock and its structure' revealed by rock, mineral and fossil specimens, models and graphics. Visitors should 'move backwards as the familiar map of Scotland transforms through video disks into unfamiliar maps of past times, and experience these environments for themselves'. The relatively small exhibition would be supplemented by a replica of part of a coal forest and a video-disk programme. Natural History proposed a diorama showing climate and vegetation with some of the more spectacular species of mammals and birds lost after the arrival of humans, followed by further timebands up to AD 1100 and 1700. The display from 1700 to the

31

Some of the material displayed in 'The Wealth of a Nation' exhibition, 1989.

present would illustrate, from Scottish specimens available, the macrofauna lost and the macrofauna gained. The 'Kingdom' display would show distinctively Scottish material, and reflect the country's contacts with the continent and England at different times. Major events discernible through the surviving material culture – the great upheavals in religion in the sixteenth and seventeenth centuries, and Scotland's emergence as a nation state – would provide a focus.[49]

Exhibition brief development continued during 1988, and some of the results were included in the immensely popular 'Wealth of a Nation' exhibition in 1989. The exhibition was the first large-scale test of the interrelationship of objects and ideas, and it raised new questions – not least the extent to which newly completed galleries in the Royal Museum dealing with specific themes could be plundered, and objects taken out of context into the new museum.[50] Jenni Calder, who edited the exhibition catalogue, and later became the Museum of Scotland script co-ordinator, was then requested to pull together the curators' proposals into coherence, with sequence, context and references. Having written extensively on Scotland's past, she had strong views about the likely visitor perception. For example, was it right to ignore critical periods of Scottish history even if the collections tended not to support them? Should, for example, Mary, Queen of Scots' jewellery be in a display about Renaissance jewellery or in one about Mary Stewart? She concluded that the public expectation would tend toward the queen rather than her context.[51] She had the support of the Director. Anderson, himself a collections man who had tenaciously clung onto the concept of study galleries, nonetheless veered toward narrative even where the collections did not appear to sustain it: 'Have we moved too far away from history? I can detect huge historical events, even periods, in the [draft exhibition brief]. I frequently mention the problem of the Enlightenment, saying that at least it must be mentioned. But where would that be? …. We are missing out. We are not treating the history of Fine Art and architecture. There is a distinctiveness in architecture. Recent RIAS exhibitions bring this out clearly …. '[52] He was referring to the then current Edinburgh Festival exhibition 'The Architecture of the Scottish Renaissance'. The task was to match academic and public expectation with the actual collections.

But what constituted Scottish? An irritated Director memorialised: 'The fact that the Boulton & Watt engine was made for an English brewery is not that important. Surely we are not intending to be that racially pure in the Museum of Scotland? Watt is one of Scotland's greatest sons …. To show the Boulton & Watt elsewhere than in the museum can be intellectually justified, but to the public it would seem capricious.'[53] Anderson further intended to use the Boulton & Watt to demonstrate that however innovative it had been, steam power remained a minority source of power in Scotland for long thereafter.[54]

The idea of Scotland, and how to display it, was a wholly new concept conceived only in 1987. At the time of the architectural competition in 1991 it was still in its infancy. The infant – in the form of a preliminary draft exhibition brief – was exposed to a senate of acknowledged experts, historians and exhibition designers on Mayday 1991. Some thirty staff and nine outsiders debated the toss vigorously, although – given that the competition was already running – the option of abandoning the child upon a barren hillside was no longer available. The senators were puzzled as to why so many messages aimed at dispelling preconceptions about uncultured Scots seemed so negatively framed. They commented upon the potential conflict between communicating the inherent values of the objects on the one hand, and 'trying to pull together the "notion" of Scotland' on the other, and enquired whether the objects were sufficient to sustain the narrative. Rather than allaying the curators' anxieties, the seminar had reinforced some of them.[55]

## The competition brief

The brief finally issued to competitors was nonetheless comparatively short and straightforward. The new building was to display the extensive national collections of objects relating to Scotland, in a way that would be enjoyable, readily accessible and comprehensible to the general public.[56] It was to include a library of some 55,000 volumes, an information centre, catering and restaurant facilities, staff offices and meeting rooms. Although it had to be fully integrated with the Royal Museum, the new museum should not 'be thought of, or appear to be, merely an extension of the existing building; it should be a distinct exhibition building for the Scottish collections of the NMS'. The requirement to be accessible to everybody presented a formidable challenge, given the Royal Museum's great flight of steps.[57]

Core displays, occupying about three-quarters of the 7000 m² of display space which the feasibility study indicated could be made available, should provide a coherent story of Scotland from the earliest geological times to the present day. Space was allocated, approximately, 5% each to geology and the natural history of Scotland, 30% to prehistoric and early historic Scotland, 20% to medieval Scotland, and 40% to modern Scotland. Displays would vary from delicate art objects to heavy industrial machines, from the ornamental to the functional, with striking variations in scale. Objects highlighted in the brief included a slab of fossil footprints, another with fossil water scorpions; major stones including the colossal Hilton of Cadboll slab; the ceiling from the Guthrie aisle; the Maiden (the Scots beheading machine imported by the Earl of Morton from Halifax, who had the privilege of being an early victim); a preaching tent; the 1830s cast-iron lantern from Girdle Ness Lighthouse by Aberdeen; and the 1617 painted ceiling from a room in Rossend Castle.[58] Some objects were sufficiently large to require special treatment: the Boulton & Watt steam engine (accompanied by a vibration warning if operated);

Photograph of the stone from Hilton of Cadboll, the largest of the prehistoric standing stones destined for the Museum of Scotland, circulated to the competitors.

Mantelpiece of the
Hamilton Palace
Drawing Room –
one of the few portions
that could be reliably
attributed to the early
18th century.

Opposite:
View through the west
end of the Hawthornden
Court to the east gable
of Greyfriars Church.

the complete wall panelling from the drawing room of Hamilton Palace, assumed to date from 1701; the 7.6 m waterwheel; the 1861 Ellesmere locomotive; and the Newcomen engine.

Although Anderson had reiterated the need for flexibility in the building's plan, the brief's statement that the core displays of Scottish material were expected to have the relatively long lifespans of, say, twenty years, gave a strong signal that the NMS anticipated permanence in the bulk of its exhibitions.[59] Subsidiary displays, particularly those in the two 250 m² galleries, might be changed more frequently. Provision had to be made for the collections to grow as the museum sought 'to maintain representation of the developing culture of Scotland'. The brief required good orientation and information for visitors, particularly at the entrance and reception areas. Environmental norms – 18°C plus or minus 2 degrees, relative humidity of 50% plus or minus 5%, air filtration of 1-2 microns – were acknowledged,[60] but the brief also expected the design to achieve high standards of energy efficiency which in the end led to a relaxation in the controls.[61] Direct sunlight, being particularly damaging, should not reach the museum exhibits.

The aspiration to fix the building tightly into Edinburgh had been part of the mindset from the beginning. The very first item at the first Museum of Scotland Exhibition sub-committee was a contemplation on 'how the building might incorporate views of Arthur's Seat, Greyfriars Kirk, the remains of the Flodden Wall, and the geological formations exposed in the NMS'.[62] Site specificity was implied not only by the requirement that the exhibition should relate to its surroundings, but in the attention drawn to the splendid views of Edinburgh Castle at roof level, and the partially obstructed view of Arthur's Seat and Salisbury Crag. This aspect had been given considerable prominence in the draft exhibition brief: 'Our aim is to ensure that the exhibition relates to the environment outside, both to the immediate environment of Edinburgh, and to Scotland as a whole. We expect there to be many opportunities to do this, literally through windows, visually through photographs and graphics, and metaphorically through context and information. We intend, wherever it is helpful and appropriate, to incorporate reference in a variety of ways to locations, sites and institutions which complement our displays.'[63] In the brief, this desire to have the city included as part of the museum experience, however, had been pasteurised down to the unexceptional hope that the winning design might 'respect and enhance the strong and distinctive cultural qualities of the capital city of Edinburgh'.[64] They feared that too much emphasis on this could lead to an inflexible design.

The feasibility study had followed the Cramond recommendations for a restaurant on the upper floors 'to take advantage of the views over the city' and that it 'might be opened at times when the rest of the building is closed to the public'.[65] In *A New Museum of Scotland* Robert Anderson had looked forward, once again, to 'a

34

restaurant – maybe one with a wonderful view over Heriot's Hospital, Greyfriars Kirk and the Castle'[66] and trusted that the design would exploit the stunning views from the north-west corner of the building. 'Rooftop restaurant', an easy concept that can conjure up the lamented roof garden restaurant that used to cap Derry & Thoms in Kensington, implies that the fundamental is the view. In another dilution of Cramond's recommendations, the brief required a restaurant without specifying location. The restaurant in the winning scheme is not on the roof, but nonetheless enjoys all the qualities of view to the castle, to St Giles and to Heriot's. It occupies a second storey slice of the museum's north curtain with a pleasant roof terrace.

These stipulations about the relationship between the displays, the building, and the environs of Edinburgh, and the brief statement that views of the outside world from inside were highly desirable, required the building to be highly site-specific.[67] Given that it was also expected to 'animate' the contents within, and that some objects 'might require or lend themselves to special architectural treatment' because of their scale or visual presence, it would be fair to infer, as did the architects, that the Trustees of the Museum desired the building to be object-specific – albeit bearing in mind the Director's reiterated desire for internal flexibility.[68] Site, artefacts and architecture should synthesise: each contributing to the other. The extent to which these ambitions were fully appreciated by the curators is unclear. The brief further suggested that some of the engineering or architectural material might be incorporated in the very fabric of the building itself,[69] as had been the case in the Burrell. The exhibition brief was still in mid-development during the competition. A fuller early draft was ready to influence the second stage competitors; but whereas the winning scheme inevitably influenced the development of the displays,[70] fully worked out display intentions were not ready early enough to influence the building's concept.

## Notes

1 Joint letter to Miss J L Ross at the SED from Hugh Macandrew, Charles Waterston, Dale Idiens, David Clarke and Allen Simpson, 12.5.1983.
2 Museums Advisory Board, miscellaneous papers 84.1 12.5.1984.
3 Interview with Sir Robert Smith.
4 Ibid.
5 'Museums Advisory Board Report to the Secretary of State', appendix 3.
6 Ibid, 1.4 and 1.7.
7 Ibid, 4.11. The result was that in 1989 the NMS established a Twentieth-Century Working Group with outside advisers.
8 Ibid 2.3. During the making of the museum, this dichotomy was to be addressed by popular input from testbeds, surveys and the Junior Board of schoolchildren on the one hand, and the scrutiny of a committee of leading historians and archaeologists on the other.
9 Ibid, 5.4.
10 To address which, an award-winning storage, research and conservation centre designed by Reiach and Hall was opened in West Granton in 1995.
11 Ibid, 1.9.
12 Ibid, 4.20.
13 Ibid, 4.28.
14 Ibid, 4.24.
15 Ibid, 4.23.
16 Ibid, 1.7.
17 Ibid, section 5.
18 Now site of the North Holyrood project and the Scottish Parliament.
19 Ibid, 5.3.
20 Ibid, 5.14.

21 Information from Dr Allen Simpson.

22 The decision to maintain a single entrance through the original museum proved almost immediately controversial, particularly in the Cramond Working Group. Many of its members supported Magnus Magnusson's view that a separate entrance was essential to establish 'the identity of the new development'. Indeed Iain (later Sir Iain) Noble stated that he could not support the expenditure of such a large amount of money on 'just an extension'. New Building Working Group, part 1, (NMS (87)7), minutes 1.12.1986; and memorandum from Noble 15.12.86.

23 Some of the Chinese lacquer is now exhibited in the Ivy Wu Gallery in the Royal Museum, opened 1996.

24 Ibid, 5.16.

25 Interview with Dr Robert Anderson.

26 Information from Dr Allen Simpson.

27 Museums Advisory Board Correspondence files 2.1.9/5.6.6, NMS, Director's memorandum 27.2.1985.

28 Interview with Dr Robert Anderson.

29 New Building Working Group (NBWG), part 1, 7.11.1986. The letter from the Trustees to the Secretary of State, 7.11.1986 stated: 'The Trustees were unable to accept any requirement to raise private sponsorship for a new building before any commitment in principle

30 Interview with Dr Robert Anderson.

31 Ibid.

32 Ibid.

33 Ibid.

34 Deputy Chairman of the Highlands and Islands Development Board.

35 A phrase within the New Building Working Group's brief, drafted by Lord Bute on 7 November 1986 (NBWG, part 1, 7.11.1986).

36 NBWG, part 1, 1.12.1986.

37 Ronnie Cramond to Magnus Magnusson 11.11.1986 (NBWG files).

38 NBWG, part 1 (NMS (87)7) 15.1.1987, paper from Dr Sheila Brock about user demand – in particular suggesting a restaurant with a rooftop view and an area for small receptions. NBWG, part 1, (NMS (87)7) 20.11.1987. Separate papers by the Director and Hugh Cheape examined different types of Information Centre.

39 NBWG, part 1, (NMS (87)7) 19.1.1987. The PSA's files on the aborted project twelve years earlier had, so it was claimed, been destroyed or were otherwise unavailable. However, the scheme was to provide four floors each with 3000 m² – yet Donaldson's was later rejected, allegedly because it could not provide 14,000 m². The Working Group set a target of 8500 m² just for the Scottish displays. Museums Advisory Board correspondence files 21.12.1984.

40 RSM: Joint Steering Committee files, report 18.3.1973.

41 Museums Advisory Board correspondence files 21.12.1984.

42 J A Leask had written to Nigel Pittman on 30.3.1987: 'I note the Museum Trustees were of the opinion that the competition should be limited to Scottish architects.' The Working Group disagreed wholeheartedly, see 'The Proposed Museum of Scotland' report, para 2.3.

43 Information from Dr Allen Simpson.

44 NBWG, part 1, correspondence, letter from Lord Bute to the Secretary of State 3.7.1987.

45 Ibid.

46 John Richards: 'Feasibility Study The Museum of Scotland', p 7.

47 Ibid, p 6.

48 'The Proposed Museum' report, 2.5; also memo from Dr David V Clarke to the NBWG 20.10.86, p 6. It was a view to which he adhered: see chapter 7.

49 Ibid.

50 Information from Dr Allen Simpson.

51 Interview with Jenni Calder.

52 Dr Robert Anderson memorandum 1.4.1991. RIAS Competition files 2.3, Comp. a.

53 Dr Robert Anderson memorandum to Dr David Bryden 30.6.1990. Museum of Scotland Exhibition sub-committee minutes, 1990-91.

54 Interview with Dr Robert Anderson.

55 Jenni Calder: 'Notes on the Seminar 1 May 1991', written 7 May. Nine visitors – including Prof Christopher Smout, Dr Stana Nenadic, Prof Martin Kemp, Don Aldridge, and John Hume from Historic Scotland – and 30 staff took part.

56 Museum of Scotland Project: Architectural Competition Brief, para 4.2.

57 Richards' feasibility study had suggested a new entrance at approximately Chambers Street level, emerging up to the principal floor within the building.

58 The ceiling had been allocated to medieval Scotland following the Antiquaries' selection of the 1707 Act of Union as the dividing line between mediaeval and modern Scotland – in the days when Scotland was still perceived as never having enjoyed a renaissance.

59 Ibid, para 4.5.

60 Ibid.

61 Information from Ian Hooper.

62 Museum of Scotland Exhibition sub-committee minutes 22.2.1990. Also 'The Proposed Museum', 3.3 (iv).

63 Exhibition Brief, second stage draft, (nd), introduction.

64 Competition Brief, 1.5.

65 Richards: 'Feasibility', para 21; also 'The Proposed Museum', 3.3.4.

66 National Museums of Scotland: A new Museum for Scotland, p 41.

67 Competition Brief, 4.6.

68 Interview with Dr Robert Anderson.

69 Competition Brief, 5.15.

70 Information from Ian Hooper.

# Unfinished business – or a case for identity

On 16 January 1990, Ian Lang, Minister of State at the Scottish Office, finally confirmed that the government would provide the money for the creation of a new Museum of Scotland on the Chambers Street site,[1] as his superior, the Secretary of State for Scotland, Malcolm Rifkind, had implied at the opening of 'The Wealth of a Nation' exhibition the previous June. The government had taken four years to reach the point anticipated by the House of Lords a long while back, but had it changed its mind? As had been the case a decade earlier, much was made of the nationalist card – that the government was using the new museum to address its plummeting standing north of the Border. Yet it seems just as probable that Bute and his team had indeed succeeded in creating a popular demand for the building that politicians found it increasingly difficult to ignore. Pressure had been sustained by the 'St Andrew' brochure, 'The Wealth of a Nation' exhibition and book, and countless presentations. All conditions demanded by the Secretary of State back in 1986 had been met. Even plans for raising private sector finance for fitting out were in hand. Rifkind's bluff had been well called. The Eighties boom had made the government wealthy, the next slump – so far as Scotland was concerned – was still almost a year away, and the Secretary of State had been faced with irresistible peer pressure.

The Museum of Scotland was to complete the Scottish cultural provision, to stand alongside the National Galleries, the Scottish National Portrait Gallery, and the Scottish National Gallery of Modern Art. But its title had deeper resonance for it knocked against the matter of Scottish identity. Lord Perth, an enthusiastic proponent of the name 'Museum of Scotland' ever since his membership of the Williams Committee, fought tenaciously in the Lords both for the title (their Lordships indulged his 'particular interest in the name') and for the necessity of the NMS to have regard for things Scottish – even though the government considered such amendments unnecessary.[2] The Lords were concerned lest the amendment might encourage a 'chauvinist approach', but in the light of a further Perth amendment emphasising that the new museum could include any or all objects in the collections from both museums, they concluded that it should not.[3]

The implications of designing a building to encapsulate national identity were not lost on the winning architects. On the original competition drawings, Benson + Forsyth had not just anchored their building to its site, emphasising the views to the Castle and Chambers Street, but had adorned the design with sources of intensely

> **For God's sake, sir, let us remain as nature made us, Englishmen, Irishmen and Scotchmen, with something like the impress of our several countries upon each!**
>
> Sir Walter Scott,
> *Letters of Malachi Malagrowther* 1826

Opposite:
St Andrew, Scotland's patron saint, with the *Renaissance* gallery beyond.
*Niall Hendrie*

Dunstaffnage Castle, from Forsyth's *Beauties of Scotland*, 1805. Dunstaffnage was an acknowledged influence on Benson + Forsyth's design.

The Museum of Scotland tower seen from George IV bridge, with the 'tower' of galleries rising above the curtain wall to the rear.
*Charles McKean*

Scots inspiration – tower houses, brochs, the standing stones of Callanish, views and details of Edinburgh, and various objects from the collections that had inspired them. The most significant photograph on their entry was of Dunstaffnage, underlining the broad formal resemblance of the castle's curtain wall, round tower and later tower-house to the way they had organised their design. Their higher tower of stacked exhibition galleries, enclosed by a lower 'curtain wall' of study galleries, ancillary uses, stairs and skylit courtyard, produced a form intriguingly similar to Gàidhealtachd medieval curtain-walled strongholds. They also provided tempting indications of how the water wheel, the Hamilton Palace drawing room, the steam engine, and some standing stones, might be incorporated within the fabric of the building itself.

The Scottishness of the design is signalled by the stone façade – though applied wholly uncharacteristically.[4] Furthermore, the massing of the museum, the relationship with its drum tower, and the detail of some of the windows, abstracts from Scots precedent. The smooth, tactile Clashach stone echoes the ashlar – the polished squared stone – of the principal façade of Scotland's most important Renaissance structures

such as Parliament House, George Heriot's Hospital, or Holyrood; and the contrast between the stone curtain and the white concrete or harled mass behind, best appreciated from Bristo Port, echoes the Renaissance contrast between dressed stone façades and harled flanks. It is not a 'Scottishness' of spurious crowsteps or corbels in the Lorimer tradition; it is a Scottishness of abstract geometries in the tradition of Charles Rennie Mackintosh.

These explicitly 'Scottish' characteristics became the principal selling point of the museum both to the public and to the Heritage Lottery Fund in January 1995. 'The design derives in part from castle architecture: the main core galleries forming the keep, and the outer building with its heavy external stonework a surrounding curtain wall. The circular tower in the north-west corner echoes the form of Edinburgh Castle's half-moon battery, which will be visible from the tower rooms, and from the roof of the new Museum .... The exterior walls will be of Clashach sandstone from Morayshire, with details in red Corsehill sandstone from Dumfriesshire, each selected for its qualities and durability of colour.'[5] Despite the curious architectural interpretation – there are few 'keeps' in Scotland (did they mean a tower-house?), and there is scant resemblance between the low billowing thickset rubbly half-moon battery and the formidably smooth drum tower – the Lottery was persuaded. Yet by implying that the character of the building was composed of an eclectic build-up of pieces from Scottish architectural history, the description misleads. The design (see 'The scheme that won', page 71) was the logical consequence of function, site, sightlines, levels and townscape: only its expression contained elements of cultural memory.

Now was not all this national symbolism rather extravagant for an extension to an Edinburgh museum in Venetian dress, even if intended as the container of the Scottish collections? A national museum does not necessarily mean a museum of a national identity. 'By a national museum is meant a museum in a capital city open to the public gratuitously ... independent of private, collegiate or society museums,' as the Lord Provost of Edinburgh was advised in 1849.[6] It had been the Williams Committee's attempt to popularise the NMAS collections that led to their rechristening as the 'Museum of Scotland' and it had felt rather smug about the idea: 'This name should have immediate appeal .... The new Museum should be more than a repository for collections satisfactorily catalogued, conserved and researched. We expect it to contribute greatly to the interpretation of Scottish culture, and to be a magnet for visitors to Edinburgh, and educational groups of all ages who want to learn about Scottish history .... Accordingly ... the status of the renamed NMAS should rise correspondingly.'[7]

The notion that the Museum of Scotland should embrace solely the NMAS's collections began to evaporate once people savoured the implications of the title. When opening the 'John Michael Wright' exhibition in July 1982, Lord Bute had referred to the proposed Museum of Scotland as 'a sanctuary of national pride', thereby considerably upping the stakes for a mere museum. The Council for Museums and Galleries in Scotland weighed in to propose that the building should 'present distinctive or outstanding aspects of the national culture',[8] without examining whether the existing collection was up to it. Once the decision had been taken to merge the two museums, the group of senior RSM/NMAS and National Galleries of Scotland staff who had welcomed the opportunities provided by a single museum, emphasised that its displays would have to incorporate objects of Scottish relevance from far beyond the NMAS collections if it were to aspire to relate 'the achievements and aspirations of the Scots in all disciplines'.[9]

Generally, museums curate, present and interpret collections. However, the Williams Committee must have had something different in mind, for it had stated: 'Scotland remains without an institution which can adequately present to its people and visitors material evidence of Scottish history and culture. This is a true measure of national poverty',[10] from which it was but only a short step for the new museum to represent the national culture. Into this trap fell the Secretary of State

The Hawthornden Court, a 'magnet for visitors'.

41

by referring to the proposed Museum of Scotland as 'the prime repository for artefacts *representing* the cultural history of Scotland',[11] when he decided in favour of a single museum under a single Board of Trustees in 1983. This endorsement of the museum as representing the country's culture – a point observed with approval in the Lords – might have been an easier task had it been begun earlier, like, say, the National Museum of Danish History, founded over 100 years earlier. The results of more than a century of a national collecting policy were more likely to represent the evolution of a national culture than two dedicated collections formed for different reasons. There were bound to be gaps. Representation of a national history to its people, moreover, signified a considerable conceptual shift from a scholarly research institute displaying its collections and making only residual provision for the 'ordinary sightseer and visitor' as had been the NMAS objective in 1951. Furthermore, a museum with a specific cultural agenda implied organisation along a chronological storyline, as the Cramond Group was later to discover.

When the Museums Advisory Board (MAB) first met, on 2 May 1984, Bute sought to dampen speculation by observing that 'the new Museum is neither a title nor a building, but a concept to be developed'.[12] His first priority was the creation of a single museum structure from the shotgun marriage of two institutions of fundamentally different personalities and philosophy. The pibroch strain of the 'sanctuary of national pride' receded behind a more prosaic tune, but every time the content of the building was considered it inevitably emerged. Collections were now evaluated in the light of how they could contribute to 'a coherent display of material illuminating Scottish culture and history,'[13] or to 'displays focusing on the history and culture of Scotland'.[14] The very title of the new museum organisation had proved contentious. Some Lords had wanted the title 'Museum of Scotland' to embrace the entire operation. The National Museums of Scotland was a smart compromise.

Once the NMS had settled down, however, the national purpose of the proposed building regained priority, and dominated work on exhibition development. Confidence grew. Robert Anderson boasted that 'no museum has presented a national history in Scotland or indeed in the United Kingdom',[15] implying that the new one would. When Michael Forsyth was appointed Minister of State for the Scottish Office, Lord Bute wrote to inform him that 'we all consider that a new building in which to proclaim Scotland's past and present is absolutely vital'.[16] The implications of 'proclaim' were picked up in John Richard's 'Feasibility Study' (August 1989): 'A new national museum will be seen as a symbol of national identity'[17] – even though the notional design illustrated within seemed scarcely to pick up the challenge. The architectural brief finally issued in 1991 implied that a comprehensive history of Scotland was to be fashioned by and within the new building. That Robert Anderson could in 1990 state that 'we considered every

Scottish or Scottish-orientated object as a potential resource',[18] was an indication, on the one hand, that the passage toward unity between the NMS collections was being won; equally it signalled a much stronger Scottish dimension to the project than had been anticipated by the MAB.

Once the National Museums of Scotland had been running for a few years, it was inevitable that the primary objective of the MAB to reinforce the unity of the new museum institution might diminish; but the determination to have only one entrance through the original Royal Museum entrance still remained. Richards had proposed to lower the entrance to a new door at basement level, to avoid the obstacle presented by the great flight of steps. Yet when these subtleties came to be addressed in the competition brief, the relationship between old and new had become very ambiguous, bearing all the signs of a compromise committee document. For whereas the new building 'should have a distinct identity', it had still to 'complement the existing Museum buildings, and avoid compromising their qualities'.[19] Moreover, the requirement for unity through a single entrance had been diluted to the flaccid 'the Trustees see merit in having a single main entrance to the Museum complex, probably retaining the present principal public entrance'.

## The architectural competition

An exemplary act of patronage demanded the best procedures to obtain the best possible design. The quality of the building was paramount – something, as Bute said later, 'of remark and of excellence'.[20] He had consulted the Secretary of the Royal Incorporation of Architects in Scotland about the possibility of using an architectural competition back in 1984 and the idea had resurfaced in the Cramond Group, which had undertaken similar consultation. Yet the museum was becoming less enthusiastic about an international architectural competition by 1989. When John Richards presented his feasibility study, the Committee decided to select an architect 'with whom NMS staff could then work to produce a mutually satisfactory design. The selection process would involve a conceptual competition and fee competition. The competing architects would not have to produce a detailed external appearance of the building'.[21] Robert Anderson informed his Policy Development Committee in November 1989 that choosing an architect was a Trustees' matter, but that the process 'would probably involve some form of competition in terms of design and fees' in line with the government rubric of the time.[22] Bit by bit, the recommendation for an international competition was being pared down to the notion of some world-famous international architect being appointed to assist the Scots to rediscover their cultural identity. Alarms sounded throughout Edinburgh. If that was what was going to happen to the Museum of Scotland, what might not happen with a Parliament building?

The cross slab from Invergowrie with St Andrew in the background, guarding the entrance to *The Kingdom of the Scots*.

Established on 15 January 1990, the Museum of Scotland Committee was delegated the task to 'draw up a brief for a limited competition to select an architect for the project',[23] with a particular focus upon the architecture of the new building, its integration with the existing RMS building, and the degree of separateness of its displays from other NMS displays. Ian Hooper, replacing Nigel Pittman as Museum Administrator and Secretary to the Trustees (later Project Director), was instructed to get on with it, as though no previous discussions of architectural competitions had taken place.[24]

## The Grand Tour

The Committee (as befitted self-respecting patrons) accepted the need to study relevant museums abroad. Not for the first time. When the original scheme for Chambers Street was being developed in 1967, the NMAS Trustees had dispatched its Keeper and Superintending Architect to visit selected museums in Europe and America;[25] and in July 1972 senior members of the building team, together with architects and an engineer, joined the NMAS Keeper and display officer 'on a week's useful visit to Denmark and Berlin'.[26] Hooper began to plan schedules for a grand tour: far from enjoying a junket, Trustees and senior staff were to be worked ruthlessly. In six days in Europe they scrutinised seventeen museums and art galleries from Paris to Stuttgart. (Trustee Sir Nicholas Fairbairn lamented the enervatingly lethargic progress.) The Committee next met in the Willards Hotel, Washington, in the midst of a further week of travelling to Canada and the United States, during which they visited twelve more museums.

Immediately on his return, Fairbairn pre-empted Hooper by dispatching Bute an idiosyncratic reaction to his European trip entitled 'The essence of an experience in German Museums'. Considerably more spirited than the official report, it contained the following apophthegms:

> It is important that the works of God enhance the works of man. The pedestrianisation and landscaping of Chambers Street is therefore a supreme priority .... All the Museums from which urban and landscape views from within were available were thereby greatly enhanced .... It is an essential requirement of the new building that the surrounding townscape of Edinburgh, especially from the higher floors ... should be regularly and imaginatively visible. It is, after all, very central to the story of Scotland .... The new building should feature an exciting view in[wards] .... The entrance to the building is of supreme importance. Some were hard to find (Meier and Hollein), and some were dingy. Some were both. The construction of the entrance chamber is critical .... A light entrance chamber with exhibits visible should be a priority .... The design and placing of the cases and their lighting is a more important feature than the spaces themselves .... All the modern buildings were to a greater or lesser extent self-

consciously being clever or different for their own sake. This frequently resulted in their being positively ugly (Cologne) or silly (Stuttgart). While novelty and imagination are to be heartily approved, since this building is another chapter in the story of Scotland, gimmickry and the cult of the contraption should be explicitly discouraged .... The more we saw, the importance of the floor surface became evident .... It is important that all details, from light switches to doors and rails and lights, must receive meticulous consideration and be of sensitive and harmonious design. We did not see any café of cheerful or pleasant ambience .... All the shops we saw were like station bookstalls.

Fairbairn concluded that 'what was good … was thoughtfully designed to exalt and complement the displayed contents and please the eye and the sensation of the visitor. Whatever was bad was either designed thoughtlessly or to please the architect. We should exhort competitors to bear this in mind as the overriding principle'.[27] The official report, more structured and useful, but less empathetic, evaluated the processes by which each building had been obtained, and recorded lessons about professional relationships. The opening of the Art Gallery of Ontario in Toronto, for example, had been delayed by two years as the result of failure to consult local communities. The Sackler Gallery of Oriental Art in Washington had enjoyed working with James Stirling. The visitors had examined La Villette's Mediathèque, the computer-operated air conditioning system at Ontario, the audio-visual techniques of the National Museum of American History, and the light-sensitive apertures in the Institut du Monde Arabe. They pored over materials – the wooden block floor in Richard Meier's Frankfurt Museum, the polished wood and unexpected colour schemes at the Sackler, and the poor details and stained masonry of Washington's National Museum of American History. Circulation was judged excellent at Mönchengladbach and the National Gallery of Canada, but rather poor in Washington's Museum of African Art. Character, atmosphere and identity emerged as the principal preoccupation. The new Louvre felt like a very luxurious airport concourse; the large internal volume at Quai d'Orsay conveyed a sense of monumentality; Quebec's Musée de la Civilisation had an 'unfortunate front hall of great pretentiousness'; whilst the architectural detail and relationship in James Stirling's Stuttgart Staatsgalerie 'sometimes seemed merely whimsical or superficially clever'.[28]

They examined labels, signage, the qualities of space – particularly of entrance halls – the proportion of exhibition to circulation space, the quality of exhibition design, outward appearance, and how the building was changing in use. The entrance to one gallery used to be through a sunken sculpture court, now seized for a café. They encountered banal views, poor entrances, indifferent shops, exhausting ramps, confusing circulation, water tanks, intrusive utilities, and thin exhibitions; but appreciated the way the interior quadrangle at Boston's Fogg Art

Lord Bute, Chairman of NMS Trustees (right), Robert Anderson, and Trustee Sir Nicholas Fairbairn, in Frankfurt.

45

Niall Hendrie

Gallery proved effective for orientation and relaxation. There had been, in short, much to learn. Under Bute's guidance, the entire committee was changing from being clients to patrons.

They visited Joan Darragh, Project Director at the Brooklyn Museum, to study the outturn analysis of her master-planning competition.[29] Ms Darragh suggested two changes: first, her selection process failed to identify some architects who should have been included, which would be remedied by an open competition. Second, the competition rules should require the submission of rather less material from the architects, and she encouraged her visitors to include interviews with architects as part of the commissioning process. It was essential to avoid the selection of an architect temperamentally incompatible with either project or client.

## The competition process

National identity beetled upon the competition itself. Who should run it? Architectural competitions in Scotland were normally organised by the Royal Incorporation of Architects in Scotland from their base in Rutland Square, Edinburgh (to whom the Cramond Group had turned in 1987).[30] Such competitions were probably at their peak in the 1989-91 period, during which the Museum of Scotland competition was conceived, administered and judged.[31] The RIAS was deeply unenthusiastic that such an important project should be put to a limited architectural competition (competition note two, see page 53), and would publicly oppose one where no Scot could enter. The Trustees had to be coaxed into allowing native architects the opportunity to compete against the international superstars.[32]

The Edinburgh network had been swiftly on the scent. Rumours swept through the capital that the museum planned a competition from which Scots architects would be excluded, and the RIAS was beleaguered accordingly. It replied to one querulous designer 'there was a plan for a limited competition. I think the Trustees are now considering a two stage competition. We are battling hard'.[33] In summer architect Ben Tindall, a scion of the east coast professional establishment, wrote directly to Bute: 'I am not sure that a competition will provide the Museum of Scotland what I imagine it is looking for', to which Bute responded deftly on a different but most resonant point: 'Like yourself, I hope that a Scottish architect may emerge as a winner.'[34]

In early November, architect Roger Emmerson addressed the RIAS: 'There has been much speculation surrounding a possible architectural competition for the design of the Museum of Scotland .... My view is that such a competition should be open to all; firstly, to attract the very best in the world, and secondly, to give Scots the opportunity of designing a major Scottish institution'.[35] The RIAS concurred, but Trustees were divided. Bute, Sir Nicholas Fairbairn, and one or two others, particularly favoured an open international competition. The Director tended toward the relative speed and safety of a limited one, and so he visited the Royal Institute of British Architects (RIBA), meeting the Director-General Bill Rodgers and Ian Shaw, the Scots-born RIBA competitions officer.[37] RIBA could not contemplate a competition closed to English architects, and suggested that a good one might involve Eldred Evans, James Stirling, Michael Hopkins, Nicholas Grimshaw and Norman Foster. They offered to organise it. Anderson next revisited the RIAS to be faced with 'a strong case for a two-stage competition with an open first stage providing the basis for a restricted second stage'.[37] His Committee was attracted by the clarity of the latter proposal,[38] agreed to a two-stage competition, and requested RIAS to clear it with the International Union of Architects.[39] The IUA, however, had established tight rules for architectural competitions to limit the possibility of the organising country having an unfair bias. The resulting procedures were bureaucratically top-heavy, almost impossible to administer and grossly uneconomic. To have followed them, the Trustees were informed, could have doubled the timescale and the cost of the competition.

In vain did the RIAS seek to persuade the IUA of the validity, objectivity and worth of its own procedures, and despondently it advised Hooper 'no matter how sweetly we talk to them, bureaucracy rules'.[40] The NMS accordingly determined to ignore the IUA regulations leaving the RIAS to choose between upholding IUA regulations and losing the competition, or ignoring the international community.[41] In April, the President of the Norwegian architects, Ole Wiig, himself a Fellow of the RIAS, offered to use his national status to lobby the IUA bureaucrats when attending a forthcoming meeting in Montreal.[42] To no avail.

Eventually Sir Philip Dowson, now appointed as Chairman of the Assessors, jointly – if covertly – with the Secretary of the RIAS, prepared two letters directed at the RIAS Council formally laying out the conditions upon which the NMS would proceed.[43] Bute wrote additionally to the RIAS President, John Spencely, emphasising the choice: either the RIAS would agree to support the NMS, or the latter would have no alternative but to abandon the competition and proceed to appoint an architect.[44] Selection would have been regarded as a betrayal by the architects, particularly younger or lesser-known architects, who had been looking forward to a rare chance to compete on a national stage. It was a matter of Scotland versus the rest of the world. At the end of June, Scotland won. The RIAS Council agreed to support the NMS,[45] and Bute wrote to its President stating how 'highly pleased and vastly relieved' he was that the RIAS was able to undertake the administration, and offered any diplomatic support that might be necessary to assist them. 'I realise it is not easy for the RIAS to set aside the IUA rules.'[46] Nor was it. As the somewhat inelegant RIAS competition minutes observed: 'We plan to do our own thing outwith the IUA regulations. The RIBA have agreed that they will file no complaint about

Sir Philip Dowson, chairman of the assessors (centre), with Lord Bute and the Earl of Perth.

this ....'[47] In May 1991 the IUA condemned the Museum of Scotland competition as in violation on 'composition of jury and its sovereignty; the rule of anonymity, the public exhibition of all projects'.[48] Rather like the Papal Bulls against Henry VIII, it had no effect. By the time of the publication of this anathema, not only had illustrated invitations to enter appeared in newspapers and architectural magazines in, *inter alia*, Hungary, India and Japan; but 371 competition entries had been received, of which over 100 were from outside the United Kingdom.

Given the international attention now focused upon it, the NMS had to demonstrate excellence in competition process. For example, it had hoped to assess the firms' capabilities and track record by requiring the submission of a curriculum vitae with the first stage design, but that proved incompatible with maintaining entrants' anonymity.[49] Fee competition, which had stuck like a burr in the NMS's thinking following the Feasibility Study, was *prima facie* incompatible with competition on design.[50] The best building would only be obtained by choosing the best design, after which fees could be negotiated satisfactorily.[51]

## The seminar

A pre-competition seminar was held at the museum on 16 October 1990 to provide information about the direction the project was taking, and examine outstanding issues before the brief was finalised. Bute characteristically raised the temperature. This 'was much more than purely a museum adventure', he stated in his introduction. He aspired to a building 'of remark and of excellence'.[52] Peter Jones prefaced some of the findings of the grand tourists by a philosophical introduction. 'It is useful to remember that whilst buildings enable people to do things, they do things themselves. Buildings are kinds of agents, influencing and calling for adjustment in our responses; they can dominate or threaten us as well as uplift, constrain as well as generate our activities.'[53] He and his colleagues had been made 'constantly aware of the first impressions upon entry': some of which had been uncomfortable, and others downright unwelcoming. He valued the opportunity to glance inside from the street. 'Many of the disasters of which we heard resulted from inadequate briefs to the architect, undeveloped ideas by the museums, and indecisive or ill-informed Trustees.'[54] He had emerged from his travels with an abhorrence of unreachable, uncleanable, dirty, leaking, rooflights.

Much was said about the architectural competition process and the role of the winning architect. John Spencely, RIAS President, thought the state might have a duty to uncover the talents of its citizens, and praised the competition system as 'an admirable way of accelerating or assisting the process of uncovering talent'.[55] He warned against the competition forcing the architects to develop a design in too great detail before a reasonable dialogue with the clients could take place:

'Otherwise you may find yourself saddled with a scheme that, with lack of dialogue, suits nobody.'[56] The design process, being iterative, goes round in circles, 'not circles like headless chickens, but sensible circles moving from the brief to the end of the process and back again'. The process of design necessarily changes the brief as it uncovers incompatible requirements and throws up alternatives. Although competitions were good for finding the right architect, they might not necessarily be the best way of arriving at the final design. So he concluded: 'The National Museums should consciously decide that the principal object of this competition should be the choosing of an architect, and not choosing a design.'[57]

He warned the organisers that the principal complaint made about competitions was to the effect that jurors set rules and then allowed them to be broken. 'Everybody knew that you only won a competition if you broke the rules.' Yet since a good competition should nonetheless allow for feats of imagination and genius, that implied that there had to be a clear distinction between mandatory conditions, to apply at all costs, and the rest. Sir Philip Dowson compared the distinction to choosing between two paths.[58] Those proceeding up the wrong path should be disqualified. Those on the correct path should be given an indication of how far up that path the client wished to go, but architects could proceed at their own risk further along the path should they wish to do so. In the museum competition, there was a commendable lack of mandatory conditions, but a wealth of hints, implications and nudges.

Dowson elaborated on the role of the architect. 'The first thing that the architect, when he is appointed, will have to do is to review and challenge [the brief]', and the NMS should be seeking an architect who would be 'an artist who can capture the feelings that Edinburgh generates, the importance that this building will hold within the community, and the atmosphere that will be generated within the museum itself.'[59] The winning architect would need to be strongly supported, and the role of patronage was to do just that. 'But he needs to have air around him, and be given the freedom and support to spend enough time on the design aspects of his work.'[60]

Judges at work: Lord Perth, Eva Jiricna, Hans Hollein, Andy MacMillan and Robert Anderson puzzling over a contextual model.

### The black box

Ironically nicknamed the black box by NMS curators, the brief comprised a black plastic briefcase imprinted with the elevation of the Royal Museum in gold, containing the brief, the regulations, a copy of *The Wealth of a Nation*, a copy of the symposium papers *A New Museum for Scotland*, eight drawings – plans, sections and elevations; photographs of the site; photographs of selected museum items; and the competition entry form. It cost £125.

Competitors would have scoured the material in the black box for every hint or nuance of jury preference. In *The Wealth of a Nation*, for example, Magnus

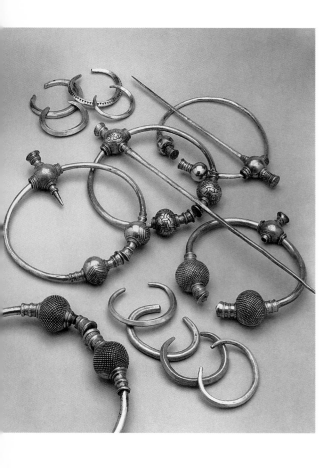

Viking jewellery from the hoards found at Skaill and Burray in Orkney, highlighting Scotland's Scandinavian connections.

Magnusson had described the NMS's collection as 'the finest and most extensive collection of Scottish material in existence' and suggested that the function of the museum should be to 'preserve and elucidate and present to the world that heritage. A national museum reflects the nation's place in the history of the wider world'.[61] He looked forward to 'a great national building in which to tell the story of Scotland's peoples'. The book's editor, Jenni Calder, described its contents – the majority of them being significant artefacts that would appear in new building – as 'a vast archive of evidence, silent witnesses to momentous events and humble domesticity'.[62] Once those artefacts were displayed in a building that matched the challenge of 'momentous', they were unlikely to remain silent.

So what else might competitors have inferred from the black box? They would have read Anderson's vision, evidently influenced by what he had observed abroad, of visitors entering an orientation area before moving up and through the core exhibition, diverting to study galleries or to areas of calm and quiet with comfortable seating. There had to be a good shop, a restaurant, views from inside out and vice versa. Its contents were predominantly but not solely Scottish, and its purpose hovered uncertainly between the passive display of Scottish collections, and the presentation of a national history.

## Assessment

Over the previous two years, the Trustees had been trauchled over the choice of assessors, particularly as to the balance between architect and non-architect, client and non-client. Partly as a consequence of the involvement of the Prince of Wales, they were determined to reserve the final decision to themselves. That meant that the competition panel would not be a 'jury' with decision-making powers, so much as assessors whose task was to determine the relevant merits of each scheme and advise the Trustees accordingly. The latter were keen to avoid accusations of having put themselves at the mercy of 'experts' (a very British fear).

They sought architectural expertise to advise them through the process, and initially considered the appointment of three architectural assessors: Sir Philip Dowson, Jane Priestman and Colin Amery. The latter was known to be close to the Prince, and the National Gallery in London had found his participation useful. Amery accepted.[63] Near-unanimous response was that Sir Philip Dowson, who had undertaken the same role in the Burrell Gallery competition almost twenty years earlier, should be Chairman of Assessors. Anderson himself had first met Dowson in the late 1960s, when acting as postgraduate client representative at St John's College, Oxford for whom Dowson was designing a new quadrangle.[64] Faxed in Sarawak with the recommendation that Dowson be Chairman of the Panel of Assessors, Bute agreed.[65] Dowson was the formidable founder and principal of the architectural practice Arup Associates, which had emerged from the engineering firm of Ove Arup and Partners. For the previous twenty years, his buildings had been amongst the most distinguished in the country. However, his firm was in the eye of the storm over the proposed redevelopment of post-war Paternoster Square, enfolding St Paul's in London, which had aborted after the intervention of the Prince of Wales.

Three architectural assessors advising the Trustees gradually metamorphosed into a Chairman – Dowson – and others to be chosen from a long list of seventeen – to which Dr Brian Hanson, the Prince of Wales' architectural advisor, added Candida Lycett Green (in the clear expectation that she would be included). Hanson wrote to Anderson on 27 June: 'His Royal Highness is far more concerned with the quality of the lay representation than the professionals on the panel.'[66] An effective competition, however, should have as few assessors as appropriate. So the NMS proceeded on the basis of indispensability, keeping firmly in view the idea (probably emanating from Bute) that professionals and laymen would be kept in balance. By the time it had included the Chairman (Bute), the Director (Anderson), the Earl of Perth, Professor Peter Jones (a philosopher with a particular knowledge of aesthetics, and Director of Edinburgh University's Institute for the Advanced Study of the Humanities), the Chairman of the Assessors (Dowson), the architect of the admired museum in Mönchengladbach (Austrian architect Hans Hollein), Eva Jiricna (Czech-born architect from London), and Professor Andy MacMillan (Head of the Mackintosh School of Architecture, Glasgow) – the jury was large enough. John Spencely attended the judging as an observer for the RIAS. With the addition of the Technical Panel, chaired by Ian Hooper, which had been appointed to advise on planning, technical, cost and users' issues, and identify any potential problems in the designs, the contribution of non-architects outweighed that of architects. In the process, Colin Amery and Candida Lycett Green had fallen along with many others.

## Launch

Two hundred applications for the brief had already been received[67] by the time the competition was formally launched in January 1991. Eventually, over 700 briefs were dispatched worldwide. The entire competition proved a sustained media event in Scotland, beginning with the brief itself. Allen Wright, Arts Editor of *The Scotsman*, welcomed the Trustees' decision to spend 1% for art, but disliked the lack of a separate entrance for the new building. He considered there was a possible conflict between 'a museum that is functionally and culturally successful ... and one that expresses its own cultural identity as a later 20th-century building, and as the Museum of Scotland'.[68]

First-stage competitors, given to 16 April to complete their entry, were limited to two A1 size boards suitable for hanging, with some brief written material. They had to demonstrate evidence of 'a design approach and capability suitable for the project.'[69] Entries were hand-delivered from Germany, France, Italy and Brussels. *The Scotsman* reported a 'last minute flood of entries, and the queue of entrants outside the RIAS headquarters, the classical town house of 1831 in Rutland Square, building up early in the morning.'[70] The RIAS headquarters had taken on the appearance of a vast postal sorting office. Three hundred and seventy-one submissions were received (365 credible ones) representing the largest overseas entry for a UK competition[71] – 50% from England and Wales, only 17% from Scotland, and the remainder from beyond. One competitor later wrote to *Building Design* enquiring how many competitors had missed the deadline 'because they were unable to open the box containing the fancy brief'.[72] Presumably only those whom one would not wish to appoint for the rather more complicated task of designing a museum.

*Niall Hendrie*

**Note one:**

Since 1979, the RIAS had been promoting architectural competitions as a means of loosening the sclerotic patterns of Scottish architectural patronage. After the slump of 1979-83, a pragmatism had entered Scottish architecture, a belief in offering the client only what he or she requested, or was prepared to pay for. In competitions lay the inspiration to higher achievement. As an experienced patron, Bute had accepted this philosophy – as he did the principal caution about the competition process: namely the possibility that it might produce a building unacceptable to the client.

By 1989 a demand had emerged amongst clients. In 1989-90 the RIAS discussed, negotiated for, developed or organised architectural competitions for a standard rural house for the Association for the Protection of Rural Scotland; developed housing competitions at Broomgate and Gallowhill in Lanark, and at Windlaw, Castlemilk; a new restaurant for the National Trust for Scotland at Inverewe Gardens; a new house at Fettes Lodge; housing in Tain and Oban; an ideas competition for the Waverley Valley in Edinburgh; the Glasgow Technology Academy (a shortlived Thatcher concept); a landscape competition for the Steelyard in Bathgate; a development plan for the University of Cyprus; a music hall for Fettes College; the John Logie Baird Centre in Glasgow; housing for the Woolwich Housing Association; new housing for the Calvay Cooperative in Easterhouse; a Weissenhof or model housing estate competition for Pilton; the reworking of Robert Adam's home as Blair Adam, Kinross; a prototype 'Scottish House' for developers; the Citadel at Ayr; rural housing in West Lothian; a prototype swimming pool for the Sports Council; and a new headquarters for Dunfermline Building Society. Of the twenty-three, thirteen went ahead, and nine were or are being built.[73]

The RIAS was also attempting to bring order to architectural competitions. Its competitions convenor, Bill Jessop, had led the rewriting of the briefs for all types of competitions and had distributed them widely amongst clients. Its procedures had received the accolade of being adopted as an appendix in the UK competition procedures document produced by the Department of the Environment. In trying to learn from the past why some competition-winning schemes had been built and others failed, the RIAS had introduced the concept of a Technical Assessment Panel in 1983. It comprised those – planners, amenity bodies, road engineers, and others – who could influence whether the scheme was built or not. The notion was that if they participated in the competition, they would be less likely to obstruct it afterwards. It also freed the competition process from having too large a jury or panel of assessors.

**Note two:**

The proposal for a limited competition was of particular concern to the RIAS. Where clients insisted upon limited competitions, the RIAS had always tried to ensure that a minimum of one-third of the entrants should be new or untried Scots architects. The logic behind this was that if one-third of the competitors had done a comparable building before, the client's interests would be safeguarded. A further one-third should be architects who had designed something of comparable complexity, but not that particular building type. Since it was important to the profession and to the country that it regenerate, one-third of the competitors should be untried architects. If the untried beat the experienced, the client could be assured that, given the technical assessment pattern, the risk was no greater. Clients had generally accepted that position.

**Note three:**

IUA regulations required the translation of the conditions into several languages; insisted upon a lengthened timescale of approval; and required jurors to be selected pro-rata to the country of origin of the entrants. That could only be determined once entries had been submitted. That caused two fundamental problems: firstly, entries are meant to be anonymous, and organisers could not ascertain the nationality of a competitor without opening the envelopes, thus breaking the seal of anonymity early. Secondly, the attraction of eminent assessors is a principal method of enticing architects to compete. If they were appointed only after competitors had submitted, there could be a slump in entrants.

**Note four:**

Two days after the launch of the competition, the RIBA Competitions Officer, Ian Shaw, wrote to the RIAS: 'As we are party to the IUA, it follows therefore that you could not say that the competition is RIBA-approved. I recall that the last Scottish international competition of significance, that in Iona, was also not RIBA approved. I wonder why this is? Does Scotland simply not bother, or deliberately disregard the IUA?'[74] The RIAS Secretary dispatched a quick response: 'The IUA will not recognise the RIAS; and, as a consequence, it does not seem encumbent upon us to seek IUA approval for our competition .... Secondly, although the competition is not formally IUA-approved, our two presidents have talked together to ensure that the RIBA would not object ....' An answer not unlike the threnody of the miller of Dee: 'I care for nobody, no, not I, if nobody cares for me ....' Three days later, a riposte: 'The IUA recognises the United Kingdom. Scotland, as Wales and Northern Ireland, is a part of the UK .... As a fellow Scot, you know that I appreciate the Scottish interest and position .... What I am not clear about, again as a Scot, is whether you believe that, at the most, Scotland should be a separate EEC member ....' No answer.

**Note five:**

Lord Bute was the President of the National Trust for Scotland and a keen proponent of a new restaurant in Inverewe Gardens, Wester Ross. A design by the appointed architect, Ian Begg, was put aside for an architectural competition, which attracted many entries. Unfortunately, the brief had contained incompatibilities and particular restrictions – one relating to the site. The preferred scheme by Richard Murphy extended beyond the approved site, and therefore could not be awarded first prize, so none was awarded. Six shortlisted architects were asked to resubmit, after which the Murphy scheme was selected. But the impetus for the scheme had dissipated, client dissension became more pronounced, Bute became very ill, and the project finally foundered on alleged grounds of cost. It ultimately transpired that the site restriction in the brief, which had prevented the Murphy scheme winning at the outset, need never have been mandatory. A different building by Sandy Gracie was erected after Bute's death.

## Notes

1 Item 12, 2.3.1990, the Museum of Scotland Trustees Committee, parts 1 and 2
2 *Hansard* 12.3.1985, pp 844-927.
3 Ibid.
4 The stone walls of the Museum of Scotland take the form of a rain screen with open rather than mortared joints, instead of the solid masonry promised in the competition entry.
5 Application to Heritage Lottery Fund, p 8.
6 Charles D Waterston: *Collections in Context*, pp 83-5.
7 Williams Report, appendix IV, para 5.
8 NMS Williams Committee miscellaneous papers, file 5.6.6 (1980-84), letter 2.9.1983.
9 Joint letter to Miss J L Ross at the SED from Hugh Macandrew, Charles Waterston, Dale Idiens, David Clarke and Allen Simpson, 12.5.1983.
10 Williams Report, appendix IV, para 6.
11 Williams Report, 2.6.
12 Museums Advisory Board miscellaneous papers 84.1, minutes 2.5.1984.
13 Museums Advisory Board Report to the Secretary of State, para 4.23.
14 Ibid, para 1.9, p 4.
15 'Scotland's history in the National Museum of Scotland' in T Ambrose (ed): *Presenting Scotland's Story*, p 65.
16 Lord Bute to Michael Forsyth 3.7.1987 (NBWG, part 1, correspondence).
17 Richards: 'Feasibility', introduction, p 1.
18 Dr Robert Anderson: 'Meeting Public Needs' in *A new Museum of Scotland*, p 41
19 Competition Brief, 3.26.
20 *A new Museum of Scotland*, p 7. Repeated to *The Scotsman*, 16.4.1991.
21 MoS Policy Development Committee minutes 21.11.1989. 'Choosing an architect would be up to the Trustees, but would probably involve some form of competition in terms of design and fees.'
22 Ibid 12.12.1989.
23 Ibid 15.1.1990.
24 NMS Trustees minutes 13.10.1990; also interview with Ian Hooper.
25 NBWG minutes 26.1.87 Paper 4: 'History of the New Museum Building'.
26 Ibid.
27 Sent to Bute 23.3.1990. Fairbairn had said: 'I found the general lethargy of our progression in Germany extremely and unnecessarily tiring'; and Anderson had repudiated the allegation of a lax and lazy trip by emphasising just how much they had seen. The implication is of a battle between instant judgements and others.
28 NMS (90) 6, Annex: 'Report of Visit to Museums in France and Germany' conflated with MoS (90) 9, Annex: 'Visit to Museums in Eastern Canada and the USA.'
29 MoS (90) 9, Annex B.
30 Visit of RIAS Secretary Charles McKean to NBWG 26.1.1987, and subsequent meetings with Anderson and Pittman.
31 The RIAS Competitions Unit was negotiating for, or organising, 23 different competitions of radically varying nature and location (see Competition Note 1).
32 RIAS Competition files 2.3 Comp. a, 1998-1991, minutes 23.3.1990.

33 Architect Ben Tindall had written to Dr Robert Anderson on 21 February seeking information about rumours of a limited competition. The reply from Willie Anthony, Building Manager, did not deny the possibility. It stated that he hoped to be in a position by June or July to 'to invite applications'. Assuming that invitations would go to the likes of I M Pei rather than himself, Tindall wrote to the RIAS on 2 March, and received the response quoted from McKean three days later.

34 Tindall to Bute 25.7.1990 (BT 009, file B 212.1); Bute to Tindall 8.8.1990.

35 RIAS 2.3 Comp. a, 19.11.1990.

36 MOS (90) 4, note of meeting with RIBA 1.2.90.

37 Ibid.

38 Although Lord Perth sought confirmation that if the RIAS were appointed, they would still be willing to listen to advice from London should it be required.

39 MOS (90) second meeting (item 3c, minutes 5.2.90). The meeting had been with McKean and Bill Jessop, the RIAS Competitions Convenor.

40 RIAS 2.3 Comp. a., McKean to Hooper 16.3.1990.

41 The RIAS then proposed a compromise of an open United Kingdom competition, with a particular invitation to four overseas architects, which was rejected as restrictive and rather unsuitable.

42 Ibid, memo McKean to Jessop 13.4.1990.

43 Ibid, Sir Philip Dowson to McKean 14.6.1990; and McKean to Jessop the following day.

44 NMS Trustees Committee minutes, part 1, Bute to John Spencely 9.7.1990: 'I think you should not be in any doubt but that the assessment process will be carried out equitably and with integrity, and I reiterate that the objectives of the Board are that the selection process should produce the best architect and the best design.'

45 RIAS Council minutes, June 1990.

46 RIAS 2.3, Comp. a, Bute to Spencely 15.8.1990.

47 Ibid 21.1.90, minutes. The RIBA had omitted to inform its competitions office in Leeds, which had to endure international reaction (see endnote 4).

48 IUA newsletter, May 1991.

49 RIAS 2.3, Comp. a, McKean to Hooper 13.8.1990: Confirmed RIAS Competitions minutes 7.12.1990. The solution was to keep the *c.v.* in a sealed envelope until after the assessors had made their selection on design quality.

50 RIAS Competitions policy 1989.

51 Bute was well aware of such matters, since he was in the thick of a competition for a new restaurant in the National Trust for Scotland's Inverewe Gardens, which was coming to a head in autumn 1990 – see endnote 5.

52 *A new Museum*, p 25.

53 Ibid, p 28.

54 Ibid.

55 Ibid, p 14.

56 Ibid, p 15.

57 Ibid.

58 Meeting McKean and Dowson at Royal Academy to discuss competitions' philosophy and organisation 1993.

59 *A new Museum*, p 20.

60 Ibid, p 19.

61 In Jenni Calder (ed): *The Wealth of a Nation*, introduction.

62 Ibid, Jenni Calder: 'The Scottish Collections', p 43.

63 MOS (90) 2, item a. The Trustees also decided to invite Philip Dowson and Jane Priestman as architectural assessors. Bute wrote to them on 26 March. Amery accepted 5.4.1990, reminding Bute that they had already met when he had accompanied the Prince of Wales to discuss the proposed Museum of Scotland (NMS Trustees, corr part 1).

64 Interview with Dr Robert Anderson.

65 Fax from Hotel Plaza, Sarawak 7.02.90 (MOS Trustees corr part 1).

66 Hanson to Anderson from St James' Palace 27.6.1990 (MoS Trustees corr, part 1).

67 *The Scotsman* 14.1.1991. The RIAS had successfully employed Neil Baxter Associates to market the competition internationally.

68 Ibid, Allen Wright.

69 Ibid 16.4.1991.

70 Ibid 16.4.1991.

73 RIAS 2.3 Comp. a., minutes June 1990-September 1991.

74 Ian Shaw to Kate Comfort, RIAS Head of Public Affairs, responsible for the competition, 17.1.1991; McKean to Shaw 22.1.1991; Shaw reply 25.1.1991.

# Judgement

## The matter of the Prince of Wales

The NMS set a target of £5 million to be raised from the private sector for the fitting out of the Museum of Scotland and formalised a Patrons' organisation to raise it. The Patrons' executive committee was chaired by the Earl of Perth, who invited the Prince of Wales, whom he had known for many years, to become its President. When the Prince accepted, it was a substantial boost since his participation could prove awesomely influential to an ambitious fundraising programme. The Prince threw himself enthusiastically into the role – but on the condition that he had a say in the outcome of the competition.[1] Bute and Perth were well aware of the problem that might present to the architectural profession – indicated by Dowson's recent experience with Paternoster Square, and the enthusiastic entanglement of the RIAS in the 'carbuncle controversies' of the 1980s. The RIAS had sought and received assurances that the Prince of Wales would have no role in the selection of the designer, and informed *Building Design* accordingly: 'Prince Charles will have nothing whatsoever to do with the judging.'[2] Architects relied upon the RIAS to ensure that that remained the case. Furthermore, Dowson's agreement to be Chairman of Assessors was conditional on no outsider to the published procedure being able to influence the result[3] since it would be in breach of the regulations, and a breach of trust with the competitors.

Although the NMS valued the Prince's role as President of Patrons immensely, it had not built a role for him into the competition regulations and did not intend to change them. Since he was not an assessor, his request for a say in the outcome was kept utterly secret, for it 'had to be played delicately'.[4] Perth and Bute were 'particularly anxious to avoid a carbuncle incident' and decided that as long as they acted in good faith, and created the opportunity of discussing their decisions with the Prince personally, agreement could be reached. Unfortunately, circumstances were to prevent this face-to-face discussion at the critical times.

In April 1990, a dinner was arranged for the President (the Prince) and the Patrons at Birkhall, the Queen Mother's house at Balmoral,[5] which the Trustees anticipated might provide an opportunity to explore further the 'extent to which HRH wished to be involved himself'. Bute, as Chairman, was mandated to 'make clear that the Trustees expected to decide the architect to be commissioned in the final design. However, he could suggest that HRH might wish to see the competition brief',[6] which it seems that he did. If the statements later issued to the press in August 1991 were correct, the Prince of Wales had used that dinner to express his

Opposite:
Steel reinforcements in concrete, outlining the emerging building.
*Niall Hendrie*

Lord Perth, Chairman of the Patrons' Committee, greeted by Robert Smith, Chairman of NMS Trustees, at the dinner to mark the opening of the Museum of Scotland.

misgiving that the competition process was inconsistent with his hope that as much weight be given to interested lay opinion as to 'so-called experts',[7] and that a condition of his involvement had been that he 'would have been able to have a say in the design of the building'.[8] This, as was pointed out,[9] was incompatible with the project rules. According to Colin Amery, the Prince 'made it clear on several occasions that he did not just want to be a name on the fund-raising writing paper, and that he hoped the museum would not select an architect through the closed-shop machinations of the professional Mafia'.[10] If all of this, in fact, had been true, it seems curious the Prince did not resign as President until days before the end of the process some sixteen months later. After all, the NMS position on the competition regulations had changed not at all. Furthermore, retrospective comments failed to comprehend that the desire to meet the Prince's anxiety on this point had probably lain behind Bute's determination that the judging process would, quite evidently, not be overwhelmed by architects.[11] It seems as though all parties were trying to make the plan work.

A week after the dinner, Robert Anderson informed the Trustees that the three topics discussed with the Prince had been the need to identify further overseas patrons, the future events with which he might be involved, and details of how the architect would be chosen. That was all.[12] Perhaps failing to appreciate the likely consequences of withdrawing the offer to Colin Amery to act as an architectural assessor, the NMS proceeded to involve the Prince as much as was now consistent with the competition regulations, and sent him the revised brief for comment. In November the Trustees learnt that, on the Prince's behalf, Dr Brian Hanson had agreed that Dowson, as Chairman of the Committee of Assessors, would give a presentation of the results of the first stage assessment to the Trustees, the Patrons and their President, on the morning of 26 April.[13] Perhaps the Prince's keen desire for participation in the competition could be satisfied by an event that explained and debated the aspirations and the criteria for judgement. When the time came, unfortunately, the Prince had to go abroad suddenly.[14] As proxy[15] Hanson joined some of the Trustees at the meeting, and made a number of further visits during the judging process.[16] Photographs of the six shortlisted schemes were sent to the Prince.

The judging process attracted substantial media attention. *The Glasgow Herald* considered that the assessors 'all want their name on an impressive project .... They might just be looking over their shoulders because the patrons of the National Museums of Scotland, whose idea this is, have, as their President, the architects' most famous critic Prince Charles .... Anything remotely reminiscent of carbuncles must be out'.[17] The assessors met on 16 April on the second floor of the Royal Museum, where there was adequate space to lay the drawings out: 371 entries assembled into 5 sets of 70 and one of 21. These were sifted by pairs of architects and non-architects 'with splendid debates and discussions'[18] – and by the end of the first day the bulk was winnowed down to 51. (That was the selection later exhibited in the Matthew Architecture Gallery during the Edinburgh Festival.) When they had finished, Dowson required them to go through it a second time, to ensure that their selection was 'unaffected by time and occasion'.[19] On the second day the entries were thinned to twelve, whose authors were identified and invited to make a presentation at interview, thus fulfilling the lessons the Trustees had learnt from their American trip about evaluating the architects' empathy. After interview the twelve were reduced to six. Having spent a total amount of time equivalent to two working weeks, the eight assessors, the project director and the RIAS observer had developed the common intention to ensure that the core of the eventual winner should never be eroded.[20]

The NMS, scrupulous in its observance of the mandatory conditions, was discombobulated by a sudden illness that prevented Hans Hollein attending the first-stage assessment. The conditions appeared to require the RIAS President to replace him, and a formal complaint was received from a German architect, Christoph Grossman, that he had not done so. Unaware that MacMillan was an architect, Grossman believed his own design would have been shortlisted if only there had been sufficient architects on the jury to dominate the non-architects.[21] (A curious mirror-image of the argument that the Prince of Wales might have been happy with the selection if only there were sufficient lay jurors to dominate the 'so-called experts'.[22]) Damned if you do, damned if you don't. In fact, the strict balance between architects and non-architects earned the competition process sufficient professional credibility to attract architects, and sufficient lay credibility to retain the support of museum professionals and of the public. The Grossman objection was swiftly despatched: the rules provided for the appointment of a substitute assessor only in cases of continued or permanent inability to undertake the role[23] and Hollein had attended the second-stage assessment.

Many young architects, realising that they stood little chance of winning, had entered the competition because they wished to display their talent to the world. The first stage had attracted some famous and soon to be famous entrants including Moshie Safdie, Daniel Liebeskind, and Chris Wilkinson. The shortlist comprised Benson + Forsyth; James Stirling, Michael Wilford & Associates with Ülrike Wilke; Michael Squire Associates; William McMorran and Simon Gatehouse; Burrell Foley Fischer; and Peter Haddon and Partners. The selection astonished the personality-cult dominated architectural papers of London, who greeted it with headlines like 'stars eclipsed in Edinburgh'.[24] Praise indeed to those who viewed competitions as a means of stimulating new talent – but that was not what *Building Design* had in mind when it sneered at the shortlist as being 'low-key since it included no international name'.[25] The names it would have preferred, or the establishment might have preferred, are implied by its promise to exhibit some twenty models of entries at a conference the RIBA was planning later that year. Models were promised from David Chipperfield, Piers Gough, Alsop Lyall & Stormer, Ron Herron, and Arup Associates.[26]

The shortlist caused equal trouble in the north. Realising that five firms were from London and one from Northampton, *Project Scotland* lamented the absence of any Scots on the shortleet: only to receive a riposte from Colin Mackenzie that Gordon Benson was not only Professor of Architecture at Strathclyde University, but had 'as filthy a Scottish accent as you could wish for'.[27]

The assessors studied the final six designs on 29 and 30 July 1991. By comparison with the first stage, the second stage judging was a very much more contemplative process. There was considerably more information on each scheme, and a model. Perth came to admire how professionals and non-professionals achieved a synthesis, for they encountered 'no great difficulty in making the selection'. Afterwards, he and Bute invited the Prince to a private meeting where they could study the drawings and models and explain them directly to him. It was precluded by the Prince's timescale so they dispatched a complete set of plans, with available photographs, and offered to explain the scheme to Dr Hanson or another architect of the Prince's choosing.[28] The offer was not taken up. By the time the committee of assessors presented their decision to the NMS Trustees on 8 August, each had received a letter from the Prince.[29] After a memorable debate, the Trustees concurred with the assessors' recommendations.

The day of the announcement of the winner, the Prince's resignation as President of Patrons was published in *The Scotsman*. He had, apparently, interrupted his Mediterranean holiday to inform the Chairman of the Trustees of his decision the previous Friday. His letter spoke of withdrawing quietly,[30] since he did not wish his resignation to be regarded as a comment on the winner, and it seemed to Bute and to Perth to be a sad but private affair, the fall-out from which could be contained. But Tuesday's *Scotsman*, carrying exclusive coverage of the resignation, contained information that could only have come from the palace. A formal statement issued from St James's Palace was statesmanlike: 'By the nature of the competitive process adopted, it has not been possible for His Royal Highness to take as active a role as he would have wished in commenting upon the design concept.'[31] He had wished, as he had always said, to play a part in the selection, but the adopted system had precluded that. Off-the-cuff comments by the St James Palace Press Secretary[32] in response to media pressure had a different slant: the Prince 'did not feel that the process was consistent with his hope that as much weight be given to interested lay opinion as so-called experts'.[33] He had failed to accept that not only had lay and expert opinion on the assessment team been balanced, but that they had also agreed on the result.

The press conference that morning to announce the winner, held in the Royal Museum of Scotland's second floor gallery, had something of the air of a carnival: a mass of press, cameras and technical machinery, and a high sense of anticipation. The world media had been so attracted by the Prince's resignation that there was a danger that the purpose of the event – the announcement of the winner – might be overshadowed. Instead they were faced with the calm assurance of Bute and Perth. The former was determined to proceed steadfastly, and on the way into the press conference reassured Ronnie Cramond: 'Since when did the House of Windsor rule taste in this country?'[34] Genially, he passed to Perth the unanticipated duty of fielding any questions about the Prince.

Architects Gordon Benson (right) and Alan Forsyth.

Bute informed the press conference that 371 first stage submissions had been received from twenty-one countries; twelve had been shortlisted and the architects interviewed; there had been six finalists and the first prize of £16,500 was awarded to Benson + Forsyth. Ülrike Wilke with James Stirling, Michael Wilford & Associates won the second prize of £14,000; and awards of £9500 each were made to Burrell Foley Fischer, Peter Haddon & Partners, McMorran & Gatehouse Architects, and Michael Squire Associates. Bute expressed the immense pleasure his fellow assessors and fellow Trustees took in the qualities of the winning design, drawing particular attention to the way it responded 'to the urban context with appropriate presence, character and massing', its circulation, its imaginative spaces and the 'creative opportunity for the displays' which it provided. The Trustees praised 'the allowance for the idea of discovery and enlightenment'. A number of matters – notably the junction between the old building and the new and the roof garden – remained to be resolved in the forthcoming dialogue between client and winning architect.[35]

The announcement of the result, the introduction of the winning architects, and the display of the model and drawings being scarcely completed, the press homed in on the Prince of Wales' resignation. They were deftly parried. In gentle understatement, Bute considered that the timing of the Prince's announcement had been 'less than ideal'.[36] Perth explained that 'Prince Charles had asked if he might have a say in choosing the design for the new building. We thought that was understandable and right, but in practice it did not work. We could not supply him with all the details of the design, so he felt that it would be best for him to stand down as president.'[37] Bute expressed disappointment at his resignation, 'but as far as the design of the building is concerned, the Trustees will make up their own minds and follow their own path. In the long run, it is not going to do anybody any great harm'.[38] He stonewalled the press with urbane geniality.

When the pursuit became hot, Bute observed 'you are flogging a dead polo pony', and the press conference was closed. Journalists clustered around the winners and a discontented Sir Nicholas Fairbairn, resplendent in a cream suit,

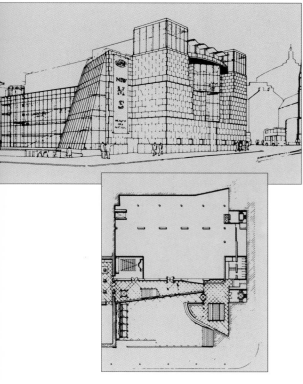

Ülrike Wilke with James Stirling,
Michael Wilford & Associates

Michael Squire Associates

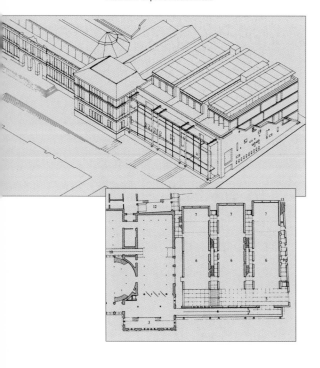

hovered over the balustrade and – unfettered by considerations of corporate responsibility – informed anybody caring to listen (and the press were not loath) that the scheme reminded him of a Mexican prison. Having enjoyed being part of the Trustees' European trip, he had felt diminished by not being an assessor. 'The Trustees were meant to have been advised right through the process. We were always promised consultation. But all the information the Trustees were told is that you can have everything from the sweet trolley as long as you have the prunes we have chosen. It is a disgrace.' He vented his discontent upon the winning design, which he regarded as a 'danger, keep out building' as opposed to a 'wonder, come-in building'.[39] The other Trustees proceeded downstairs, with those involved in organising the competition, to lunch on strawberries at smooth round tables organised in perfect hierarchy.

The media's reaction exemplified the apparent difference between Edinburgh and London, for the Prince's interventions in London had proved influential. That was certainly what *The Times*, *Sunday Times (Scotland)* and *Financial Times* expected to obtain in North Britain. *The Independent* was less certain: 'Scotland has a very different architectural tradition, and in resigning, the prince might well upset local opinion …. Scots are likely to rally round the winning design.'[40] Hugh Pearman concurred: 'The Museum is better off without him …. Edinburgh has a chance to improve its dismal record of getting good new architecture into the constipated centre.'[41]

Over the previous three months, the press had been growing increasingly exercised over the lack of public participation in the judging. Given the NMS's own aspiration to communicate more effectively with the public, the RIAS's refusal to put the six shortlisted schemes on show seemed perverse.[42] The reason it gave was that an early viewing of the shortlisted designs ran the risk of prejudicing the second-stage judging, and its past-president, John Spencely, pointed out that that similar attempts had failed in the past: 'There is a belief we can count on the general public to take sufficient interest in a building to be able to make an informed judgement. Frankly, I do not believe that is possible.'[43] The most popular designs for the previous competition projects in Edinburgh's Morrison Street and Lothian Road had both proved unbuildable, and in any case an opportunity for formal public participation would occur at the stage of planning permission. Nicholas Fairbairn concurred: 'I would not ask the public to design a bus or Edinburgh Castle, or Holyrood House, and I am suspicious of saying that what you want is a jury of the public.'[44]

The Secretary of the Royal Fine Arts Commission for Scotland thought 'it would be most eccentric if the whole world were allowed to see the shortlisted designs',[45] and a rather brusque RIAS had dismissed the notion: 'There is no point in wasting time arguing about it.'[46] You only needed to look at the outcome of the recent competition for the Dulwich Art Gallery, where the designs were published

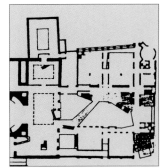

Burrell Foley Fischer

before the winner had been announced. A journalist from the *Financial Times* (Colin Amery) was alleged to have ended up 'effectively judging the competition'.[47] *The Scotsman* editorialised: 'Both sides are wrong. There could quite reasonably have been an exhibition in public or disclosure of the choice available and an explanation why rival designs were rejected [but] it would have been absurd for the lay public to be presented with 400 entries, or even 12, from which to choose. The result would almost certainly have been a compromise, probably a disaster.' To judge by some of the questions at the press conference, the apparent exclusion of the public still rankled. Bute's response was characteristically amiable: 'In a sense, this is the beginning ... now the competition process has been completed, we will again be taking exhaustive consultation as the design develops over the next 18 months to 2 years.'[48]

A week later, Colin Amery attacked in the *Financial Times*. He deplored the Prince's marginalisation by the Scottish establishment and presented a highly selective version of the saga. 'Despite being President of the Patrons, HRH The Prince of Wales was only shown some black and white photographs of the final six just before the announcement of the winner',[49] as though, even had that been entirely so, that were sufficient reason for his resignation as President of Patrons. Amery's disdain for the winning architects and their scheme was palpable. He adumbrated how little they appeared to have built – an oratory (incorrectly located in Scotland) – and how their 'expensive' local authority housing had required remedial action by others. He then mocked the museum's design as a 'stylistic cross between Le Corbusier' (the Prince's principal demon) and Scottish architecture, observing that Birnam Wood appeared to have settled firmly on the roof. (His scepticism about the 'Scottishness' of the design was echoed in a sour caption in the September *Architectural Review*: 'Neo-Corbusian cliches excused as Scots archetype.') The round tower, 'surely a straight

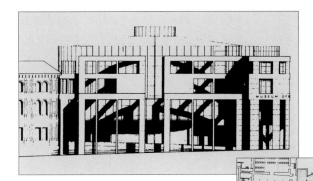

Peter Haddon & Partners

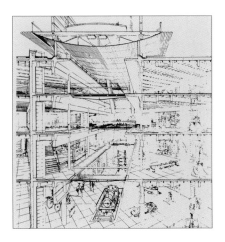

McMorran & Gatehouse

copy of work by Mario Botta, will be a bizarre addition to the Edinburgh street'. The language – 'incongruous grove of pines … abstract sculptural qualities … random windows … strangely angled projecting cornice' – was one of damnation to those conversant with the Prince's *Vision of Britain*. Not that the roof garden was altogether favoured. The Trustees were doubtful, and even the assessors themselves had been uncertain about its practicality and relevance, and did not consider it fundamental to the scheme.[50] The curators had 'disagreed very strongly' with the proposition that it should be conceived as part of the museum's displays;[51] and even the Cockburn Association had some fun at its expense. 'A roof garden is fine by us, but not if it is sitting on a flying saucer exposed to the elements …. If you submit a planning application … we will object on the grounds of inaccuracy unless the cypress trees are drawn at an angle of $45°$.'[52]

Ironically, given the arguments about public participation, entries to the Museum of Scotland received much more public display and access than the norm. The NMS displayed drawings and models of the final six, with a slide show of the shortleet of fifty-one. Edinburgh University's Matthew Architecture Gallery, across the street, exhibited forty-six of them. The largest exhibition was the third. Edinburgh architect Ben Tindall had been unhappy about the competition (although he had entered) and was even more unhappy with the result. He wrote to the RIAS:

> It is true I find it upsetting, strange and wrong that five out of the six finalists out of 360+ entries to an international competition should come from London. Is London really the world centre of architectural excellence? Is it a pure mathematical fluke? I think not. The only logical explanation is that the entries were judged against the mores of London architecture. When architecture is to be judged against London mores, then the attempts of Scottish/foreign architects will be in vain …. If there is any conspiracy, perhaps it is the Museum who appeared to want Richard Meier in the first place and chose the nearest they could get.[53]

Tindall wrote to all competitors offering to hang their first-stage entry (most of which still remained in Scotland) in a partially completed office adjacent to his own off Victoria Street, in the Old Town. Over 100 competitors agreed to take part in what became called the *Musée des Refusées*, at one drawing per practice, crammed into steep, cramped atmospheric spaces seemingly hung halfway down the back of the rock of old Edinburgh. The exhibition was marketed as 'over £1 billion pounds of architectural design in one room'.[54] The designs included those of Ian Ritchie, YRM and Ted Cullinan. It was vigorous, overcrowded, and exciting, but attracted notices that were mostly and deservedly ambivalent: 'Mixed in with some great ideas there are inevitably some real horrors, some non-starters and lots of repetition.'[55]

However, save for the judgement that the gap between the winner and the runner-up was a close-run thing, there emerged no groundswell that the assessors had made the wrong choice.

The main exhibition was not well attended by those accustomed to leaving their thoughts in visitors' books. By the following Sunday, after three days of exhibition, there were only thirty-five comments in it: twelve applauding, seven preferring the runner-up, and eight violently opposing everything.[56] *Building Design*'s reviewer, Jessica Cargill Thomson, regretted that the judges had failed to present a detailed critical appraisal, and thought it ironic, given the lack of earlier consultation, that the public was now being asked to make its own judgements. The roof continued to cause controversy. The NMS had commissioned a model which, if studied through the scope, revealed that the roof garden would be virtually invisible from street level. Unfortunately, the standard photograph of the model issued to the press was from a viewpoint above, which could only, according to the RIAS, have been enjoyed by a demented pigeon.[57] It made the roof garden seem over bulky and

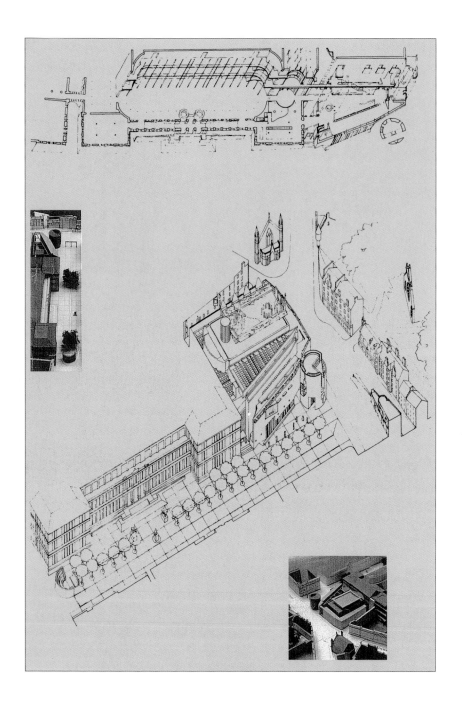

Benson + Forsyth competition drawings showing the building's relationship with the Royal Museum and its neighbours. Note particularly their proposals for the landscaping of Chambers Street.

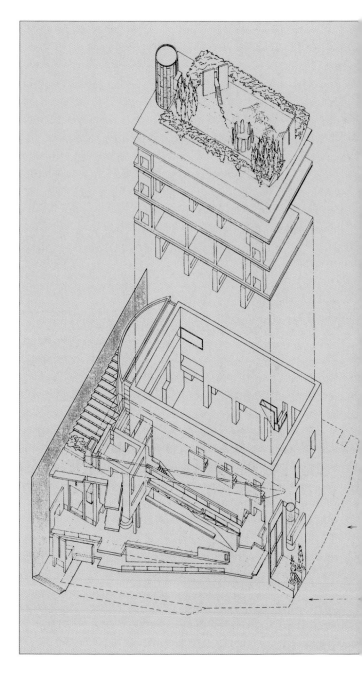

Axonometric presentation of the orientation area (Hawthornden Court) and main gallery space.

66

conveyed nothing of the interior or the streetscape. The drawings were simple black and white elevations and sections, which were arduous for non-experts to decode. Fairbairn, who, on his travels as Trustee around European museums, had shown himself a sensitive commentator on buildings, spaces and materials, had completely misread them in his analogy with Mexican prisons; and he earned a suitable riposte from *The Scotsman*: 'Sir Nicholas Fairbairn, whose acquaintance with them is happily greater than mine, recently compared prisons in Mexico to the new Museum of Scotland. He must have enjoyed his sojourns in them, for that is quite a compliment to the prison.'[58]

The emergence of the winning design presented Scotland with the first coherent idea of what the museum might be like; and a first reaction from some of those involved in, or watching, the unfolding of the idea, was focused upon how cramped it now appeared in comparison to the expansive promises of the Williams Report. Duncan MacMillan, Curator of Edinburgh University's Talbot Rice Gallery, lamented that 'Scotland is an annexe, it is not a museum of Scottish culture'.[59] Julian Spalding, then Director of Glasgow Museums and Art Galleries, could not accept that the Museum of Scotland should take the form of what he called 'a small extension'. He blamed Anderson (unfairly) for 'considerably depleting' the original plans – *ie* the Williams' Report proposals. In a ghostly reiteration of Tebble's arguments he suggested starting again on a new site with its own identity: 'The people of Scotland will find that their

rich and exciting history has been shrunk into a short sequence of galleries occupying only half of a small extension tagged on to the end of the Royal Museum.'[60] He suggested that it was only because the building had no identity of its own that its architects 'have had to dress it up in Scottish gimmicks like the lean-to broch and Ascot hat glen garden on the top'.

Three weeks later, once the dust had settled and queues had had the chance to visit the three exhibitions emanating from the competition, Henry Porter ruminated in *The Independent Magazine*: 'It is difficult to avoid the feeling that the Museum authorities in Edinburgh are pretty pleased with the outcome of this now famous dispute .... They have, after all, defeated the great supervening amateur of the Eighties, and they will now build their Museum of Scotland as they want it .... The Prince had become used to obeisance in architecture, and like many princes before him, he had failed to watch his northern border.'[61] Those who had contemplated the lineage of Crichton-Stuart (Bute) and Drummond (Perth) concluded that the decision to proceed was the final act of Culloden.

The Prince had never allowed himself to be drawn into criticising upon the design directly. Indeed, his letter of resignation stated that it could not be taken as a comment upon it. Lord Bute forecasted at the press conference in August 1991 – 'I think, in the long term, the Prince may actually like the building.'[62] In December 1998, two days after the Museum of Scotland opened, the Prince was asked for his reaction to it. He declined to make one: 'I never comment upon architecture on Wednesdays.'[63]

# Notes

1 Interview with Lord Perth. Notwithstanding the Earl of Perth's presence on the jury as chairman of the Executive Committee of the Patrons, the Prince's office later stated that the Prince's 'main official responsibility lay in ensuring that the Patrons were properly included' and that his requests for involvement in the selection of the architect were made on behalf of the body of Patrons. (Deputy Private Secretary to Mark Jones 31.8.1999.)

2 *Building Design* 19.4.1991.

3 Interview with Sir Philip Dowson: 'He had only been prepared to chair the assessors if no influence was brought to bear by people who were not amongst the assessors.'

4 Interview with Lord Perth: 'The Prince of Wales' desire was always in the background.'

5 James Meek, *The Scotsman* 14.8.1991.

6 NMS Trustees minutes 30.3.1990.

7 *The Independent* 14.8.1991.

8 *The Scotsman* 14.8.1991.

9 *The Independent* 7.9.1991.

10 Colin Amery: 'Why the Prince walked out' in *The Financial Times* 19.8.1991.

11 NMS Trustees minutes 11.4.1990. As had been made explicit from the start, in terms of the competition regulations, lay participation in the process could only lie with the non-professional members of the assessment panel. Although public opinion counts were taken during the Scottish Parliament building competition, effectively the only lay participation there, as well, was through the lay juror, Kirsty Wark. Given the immense difficulties of evaluating public opinion, perhaps the position of a lay or people's champion as one of the competition jury, could be

formalised, to whom opinions could be directed.

12 Ibid 19.11.1990. At the same meeting, Bute persuaded the Trustees to remove the 'highly restrictive tone' of the cost guidelines in the brief. 'Whilst it was reasonable to refer to the public expenditure planning figure for the project, this should not be in terms which suggest that this was an absolute cost limit which could not be exceeded in any circumstance' (*Patron at work*).

13 Ibid 19.11.1990, interview with Dr Robert Anderson.

14 The Prince's office pointed out that, in any case, such a meeting could hardly have been one involved in the decision-making process since it took place several days after the 317 entries had been weeded down to 12, 'and neither the Prince nor the Trustees were advised fully of the criteria which were used in making this drastic initial reduction'. (Deputy Private Secretary to author 31.8.1999.)

15 Interviews with Sir Philip Dowson and Dr Robert Anderson.

16 Dr Robert Anderson.

17 *The Glasgow Herald* 22.4.1991.

18 Interview with Sir Philip Dowson.

19 Ibid.

20 Ibid.

21 Letter from Christoph Grossman to President RIAS 13.05.1991.

22 As the St James' Palace Press Secretary was later to put it. (Deputy Private Secretary to author 31.8.1999.)

23 Kate Comfort to Christoph Grossman 31.5.1991.

24 *Building Design* 17.5.1991.

25 Ibid.

26 Ibid.

27 *Project Scotland* 13.6.1991 and 27.6.1991. Mackenzie was a Clydebank architect who had been job architect on the Linn Products

factory in Eaglesham by Richard Rogers. He also pointed out that Ülrike Wilke (the Mackintosh School), had married a Scot and worked for a Scot in London.

28 Interview with Lord Perth.

29 Interview with Ian Hooper.

30 The Prince's office emphasise the Prince's intention to keep his resignation discreet, so that it 'would have minimal effect on the Museum's ability to promote and raise funds for the winning scheme'. It states that the resignation was made public by the museum. (Deputy Private Secretary to Robert Smith 30.6.1999.) This delicious notion of a Machiavellian conspiracy by the NMS grandees is presumably based on the assumption that the resulting publicity would have brought far greater international attention to the press conference than otherwise might have been enjoyed. There is no evidence in the files to support it.

31 *The Independent* 14.8.1991.

32 Deputy Private Secretary to author 31.8.1999.

33 *The Independent* 14.8.1991.

34 Interview with Ronnie Cramond.

35 NMS (91) 14C.

36 *The Evening News* 13.8.1991.

37 Ibid.

38 *The Sunday Times* 18.8.1991.

39 *Daily Telegraph* 14.8.1991.

40 *The Independent* 7.9.1991.

41 *The Sunday Times* 18.8.1991.

42 James Meek: *The Scotsman* 14.8.1991.

43 John Spencely: ibid.

44 *The Sunday Times* 18.8.1991.

45 Charles Prosser: *Project Scotland* 13.6.1991.

46 Kate Comfort: ibid.

47 Ibid.

48 *The Scotsman* 14.8.1991.

49 Amery: op cit.

50 The assessors 'queried the practicality and relevance of the roof garden, which they did not consider fundamental to the scheme', NMS (91) 14.

51 'If the roof garden was concerned as part of the display proposal, the panel disagreed very strongly with both the concept and the treatment.' Ian Hooper: 'Report to the Assessors: Comments of Statutory Bodies' 5.8.1991.

52 Oliver Barratt, Secretary of the Cockburn Association, to Dr Robert Anderson 7.11.1991.

53 RIAS 2.3 Comp. a., Ben Tindall to McKean 22.8.1991. Tindall had been 'outraged at the disparity between the short listed designs and the brief requirements for prominence, respect for the street and that the contents should dominate'. He judged that the assessors had chosen by fashion, media and their own prejudices. If the results had been preconceived, months of work had been wasted. Worse, there was no planned exhibition and no feedback. He considered that the RIAS had been exploited. Since he was then doing up an office off Johnston Terrace, he obtained names and addresses of the competitors from the RIAS, and wrote to them all, offering to hang a drawing each for £20. He exhibited over 100, and it took days to hang. The number of visits from museum staff was notable. (Interview.)

54 *Building Design* 23.8.1991.

55 Ibid.

56 *The Sunday Times* 18.8.1991.

57 *The Scotsman* 14.8.1991.

58 *The Scotsman* 2.9.1991.

59 *The Scotsman* 8.10.1991.

60 *The Scotsman* 29.9.1991.

61 *The Independent* 7.9.1991.

62 *The Sunday Times* 18.8.1991.

63 *The Scotsman* 3.12.1998.

The museum rising above
the roofs and chimneys
of Candlemaker Row.

The roof taking shape,
against the background
of Arthur's Seat.

# The scheme
# that won

## The architects

Gordon Benson and Alan Forsyth were contemporary students at the Architectural Association (AA). Benson, who had taken his first degree at the Mackintosh School of Architecture in Glasgow, had been profoundly influenced by the city's canyon-like streets, their sharp edges brilliantly lit against the changing skies, by the austerity and control of 'Greek' Thomson, and by the imagination of Charles Rennie Mackintosh. But he encountered a 'smothering quality' in Scotland. 'You had to leave to breathe, since a small number of practices carried out all the interesting commissions.'[1] Forsyth was from Newcastle. To London eyes, they both therefore had a certain 'grittiness' (one of those inescapable north British characteristics). The AA was in its 'full Le Corbusier frenzy – all to do with [Alan] Colquhoun, [Colin] Rowe, socialism and fraternity. There was a balance between ideas and feelings: an emphasis on sensuous spaces – houses, the Unités, and democracy: all this was new.'[2] Both students were preoccupied with volume, light, pure form, and consistency of detail: Forsyth under the influence of Alvar Aalto, and Benson that of Le Corbusier; the seemingly disparate figure of Charles Rennie Mackintosh lingering in the memory. A visit to Corbusier's pilgrimage chapel at Ronchamp later 'reconnected Mackintosh with Corbusier'.

After graduating they joined the team led by architect Neave Brown, in the London Borough of Camden, whose architects' department had earned an international reputation for its new housing schemes. It was for the austerely beautiful and clever houses in Maiden Lane and Mansfield Road, the antithesis of the house as an agglomeration of poorly lit box-like rooms, that Benson and Forsyth first attracted notice. The houses were undoubtedly ingenious, but demanded from the occupants a certain sophistication of lifestyle.

Anticipating that it would be relatively straightforward to set up in practice, they left Camden in 1978, expecting, perhaps, a commission from their former colleagues for some more of the work at which they had shown themselves so adept. But the government had changed, and Local Authorities began their long slide into retrenchment. The one scheme, newly completed, that might have provided them with sufficient momentum for a new practice was the development of forty-two extraordinary terraced houses at Branch Hill, Hampstead. Benson + Forsyth were invited to describe it to a conference in the Sainsbury Centre, Norwich in early 1979; and after a hot summer's tour accompanied by an enthusiastic occupier with a bottle of over-warm Ballantyne's, it was duly featured in the *Times*. Branch Hill

> **" Old architecture lived because it had a purpose. Modern architecture, to be real, must not be a mere envelope without contents. "**
>
> Charles Rennie Mackintosh

was a seemingly simple vision of white terraced houses tumbling down a hillside, where the garden of one was the roof of the one below; wild romanticism burst from the white spiral stairs winding from terrace to garden.

It was no longer what the world was looking for. The world of 'culture' had discovered post-modernism. Their contacts withering, there followed the mandatory period of privation, sustained only by teaching at the AA and at Strathclyde University.

Over the next twelve years they entered sixteen competitions, won five, and were second or premiated in five more: none built, with prize money 'buttons – at best'. Other designs – a theatre on the banks of Derwentwater, Cumbria and a Science Innovation Centre in George Street, Glasgow – remained unrealised. The latter, for Strathclyde University, was like a John the Baptist to the Museum of Scotland. Its derelict site was the hinge where Glasgow's new town impinged upon the echoes of the medieval city and Robert Adam's Shuttle Street, in the former university quarter of Glasgow (which the academics had sold for a railway station a century earlier). Picking up on these references, the design emerged as blocks enclosing a triangular, roof-lit central space with the functions disposed around it. It did not proceed. In twelve years they had built a house, some interiors and studios, a workshop, and a bay of the cavernous and echoing brick vaults beneath Glasgow's Central Station for the Year of Culture's exhibition 'Glasgow's Glasgow' in 1990.

Although published twenty-six times in journals from Tokyo to Italy and France, magazine publicity feeds few mouths. *Church Building*, however, featured the Oratory at Boarbank Hall, Cumbria, a nursing home run by Augustinian nuns for whom they had already designed a physiotherapy room. The Oratory was not on the tourist trail: and what caught the imagination was the photographs of a gently translucent cylinder within a white cube, whose proportions approximated to Bramante's Tempietto at San Pietro in Monitorio, Rome. It was 'all feeling – no function'.[3] With such a hesitant record of recently built projects, the Museum of Scotland represented their best opportunity to date to design a building of national significance.

Nobody considering a new museum in Scotland could do so without some reference to the 1984 Burrell Gallery by Barry Gasson (originally designed with John Meunier and Brit Andersen): the way it framed the landscape (particularly the long glass wall facing 'The Walk'); the way it incorporated medieval doorways and seventeenth century rooms into the very fabric; and the manner in which the objects were precisely positioned within. Benson + Forsyth also admired the Italian architect Carlo Scarpa's use of position, light and context to add power to the objects on display; and they found an 'extraordinary marriage of intellect and sensuality' in Le Corbusier's monastery at La Tourette, and inspiration in his

pilgrimage chapel at Ronchamp. They shared the Japanese belief that architecture should not be too explicit: 'You don't see; you have to be made aware.'

The Museum of Scotland competition was different in kind to other competitions in the implications for the building form of the building's contents – 'objects you could hang on to' which included some of immense power. Although there was no question of either designing a monumental warehouse as a simple container, or of imposing an uncongenial work of architecture upon pieces of Scottish history, they intended to explore how location and positioning within the museum might contribute to their impact. 'An architect becomes a catalyst – a midwife – whose task is to synthesise data. Since artefacts carry messages, the task is to find the real – no matter how fragmentary.'[4]

## The setting

During the 1980s Benson and Forsyth had taught a unit at the Architectural Association School of Architecture in London, organising student projects in Edinburgh and Glasgow 'from a polyglot London base'. Against student projects that were insufficiently responsive to their site – even Branch Hill belonged to a form of what they called 'utopian placelessness', sitting in a tree-surrounded garden that could as well be at Pessac or in the Veneto as in Hampstead – they sought a location that provided 'a recognisable, shared and discussable focus'.[5]

Edinburgh had been ideal. The city was still inhabited, still accessible, visually legible, and could be treated as living history.[6] The Cowgate, in particular, was an intriguing place to develop new ideas about the role of contemporary urban architecture. Its canyon-like character, medieval ridge to the north and sunny plateau to the south, represented a particular inspiration.[7] They were fascinated by its character and contrasts: its views and vistas, hills and valleys, distant skylines and confined immediacy, light and dark, narrow closes and wide streets. The materiality of the place above all: different types and colours of stone, polished ashlar, heavy rubble, and smooth, rough and sometimes multicoloured surfaces. So when the competition for the Museum of Scotland was launched, in January 1991, they considered 'they already had the vocabulary' for such a site. Competitors who did not know Edinburgh, and could not afford sufficient time to get under its skin, would have been unable to derive comparable insight into the nature and character of Edinburgh solely from studying the brief.

Benson and Forsyth had spent almost a decade distilling their vision of what, in their opinion, was uniquely good, and uniquely flawed, about Scotland. They perceived a duality in Edinburgh's architecture: the medieval Old Town was architecture that 'had grown from the rock' organically, in contrast to the rationalist New Town which appeared imposed upon the landscape.[8] The competition site

enjoyed a 'dream site' in the valley between irrational medieval and Renaissance Edinburgh (represented by Greyfriars, the Grassmarket and the looming Castle) and rational Edinburgh symbolised by the dome of Edinburgh University: the hinge between instinctive, intuitive yet inchoate old Edinburgh, and the horizontally proportioned platonic forms of Enlightenment Edinburgh, represented by the institutions of Chambers Street.

## The competition

The assessors intended to choose an architect rather than a design, so first-stage competition submissions were taken more as an indicator of attitude, empathy and skill rather than as formal proposals. 'The panel wanted to understand each competition entry as a response to the brief.'[9] Benson + Forsyth, however,

seized the opportunity to codify and pour out all the responses that Edinburgh had generated in them over the previous decade; and developed their first-stage design to a far greater depth than was necessary – almost to the degree of a final design. They assumed that a more detailed brief would emerge for stage two; but there was to be little more than what emerged at the interviews and a very embryonic first draft exhibition brief.

All shortlisted architects received comments on their design, met some of the curators and users, and enjoyed a pleasant opportunity for some significant mutual misunderstanding. The Director reiterated that since the winning building would have a much longer life span than even the permanent exhibitions, designs would have to be sufficiently flexible to allow the possibility of radical change.[10] When Peter Jones asked Benson + Forsyth to identify the weakest point

in their design, they replied 'the impact of the exhibition design upon the building'[11] was what required most attention. Their second-stage design concentrated, therefore, upon crafting their architecture around the objects, and upon the different qualities of light and experience they hoped to create within. All they had to guide them was the draft exhibition brief. Although they brought an informed outsider's perception of cross-cultural resonance into the narrower world of discrete collections, the building programme and the exhibition design programme were out of step.

## Design generators

The principal design generator was the nature and location of the site. It was not large. Although the museum contains significantly more display space than the Burrell Gallery in Glasgow,[12] it has nothing like the footprint, and its exhibitions would have to be stacked.[13] Hence one of the glories of the new museum – the experience of moving through, up and down curving stairs, circular stairs, straight stairs, glass lifts, top-lit lightshafts, viewpoints, galleries and balconies, each reinforcing the sense of verticality and volume – is a consequence of the site. That it had also to appear as though it were only four storeys tall, in keeping with the remainder of the street, led to the development of a stone curtain-wall, slipping easily into the scale of the street concealing a seven-floored tower of galleries behind.

Critically, both the Castle Esplanade and Arthur's Seat would gaze down upon the new building's roof. Since it would have been unsophisticated to offer tourists visiting the Castle or Arthur's Seat a view of the typically grey modern flat roof cluttered with subtopian and inelegant extract ducts, lift housing, machinery and plant, there was no option but to treat the roof of the building as a 'fifth façade'.[14] Intrigued by the tension of what might be put on the roof – 'like a landscaped mound' – against Arthur's Seat rising behind, they conceived the idea of the building's skyline being occupied positively by a 'hanging glen or valley'[15] rather than by an inert feature like the University's dome. The inescapable lift shaft housing was realised as a prominent, gleaming tower whose partially stone-clad top echoes the cap house at the apex of a Scots Renaissance stairtower.

The plan derived from the resolution of three geometries: the ancient forms of buildings rising from an irregular landscape; the pure forms imposed upon Calton Hill and its neighbourhood or exemplified by the repose of William Adam's tomb; and the forms and contradictions implied by the site itself. 'Many of the contrasts are taken from the landscape and imprisoned within the building.' They wrote on their competition drawings that 'openings in the wall relate the exterior world to the interior such that the city becomes part of the exhibition. Conversely, views into the museum allow it to become part of the City.' Throughout the building there

The curved apsidal stair-
case at the east end of
the museum.
*Charles McKean*

*Niall Hendrie*

were proposed *points de vue* (the competition drawings indicated some of the historic sources such as the Renaissance oriel window facing over the sea from Gylen, on the southern tip of Kerrera). Windows faced the Castle, the McEwan Hall, the Infirmary, Provost Chambers, and there were views westwards to George Heriot's (Renaissance education) and Greyfriars (monastery, Reformation, Covenanters and death). As visitors moved through the building, they should enjoy previously unavailable vistas – 'physical postcards, as it were, of Edinburgh' – as exhibits themselves, for 'these glimpses of the outside impinging on the inside will *complete the whole show*'.[16]

The architects' reaction to the artefacts, and to the contents of *The Wealth of a Nation*, was admiration for the capacity of the people of Scotland to transform their resources and make things out of them, in a process of ceaseless renewal. They had an absolute belief in the power of architecture to lend spirituality to objects – which varied in scale from tiny medieval relics to a waterwheel – and thought that success could be measured by the extent to which the storyline could become apparent *without any text at all*. At that stage there was insufficient information about the displays to be able to form an understanding of the relationship between the parts – particularly those intended to be spiritually elevating. 'The difficulty lay in trying to extract a firm brief of ideas, spaces and experiences' particularly for the sixteenth to eighteenth centuries. It was no less difficult for the museum and the curators themselves at that stage in the concept's development (see 'Exhibition evolution', page 101).

Uninspired by 'high-tech' architecture, Benson + Forsyth compared it to body-building, lacking the ability to order and put into a hierarchy the colossal amount of information that a new building should convey. They considered it different in kind to the admirable Victorian cast-iron structure of the Royal Museum (formerly the RSM).[17] Inappropriate importance given to technology would unbalance other messages, and act as a barrier between visitors and immediate experience. Only where it added to the understanding of that space was engineering expressed in the design. Mackintosh, similarly, displayed wonderful roof trusses, but only where they formed part of the larger language of the design, and played a particular role in defining space. In spaces like 'The Reformed Church', great pains were taken to 'eradicate technology' and contemporary fixings are concealed behind wonderfully detailed stonework. Late twentieth-century window technology had no contribution to make to the sixteenth-century Reformed Church.

Whereas the 1989 Feasibility Study had proposed the 'precise and modern' materials of heavily shot blasted stainless steel panels and sheets of glass[18], Charles Rennie Mackintosh had dismissed such materials a hundred years earlier: 'Iron and glass, though eminently suitable for many purposes, will never worthily take the place of stone, because of this defect – the want of mass.'[19] By contrast, the winning

design exaggerated mass – with its hollowed-out walls, recessed windows, and protrusions seemingly extruded from the walls. Internal spaces and display niches were carved out from fat walls with deep doorways. External space was walled by the city. Although fat walls were used to provide geometry and proportion, and had the resonance of the walls of brochs, the design was the antithesis of monolithic. Pieces were carved for a function, disconnected one from the next to emphasise their identity; and then reconnected by ramps, stairs and bridges. Connections between were designed to emphasise the passage through thresholds. Exhibition spaces designed to contain objects were distinguished from non-exhibition spaces, to prevent the latter becoming 'spaces with cases'.

The vista down George IV Bridge presented a problem. It had always been hoped that the new museum would be visible from the High Street, acting as a beacon along George IV Bridge to tempt the great mass of tourists lolling up and down the Royal Mile. Had the site extended as far west as the (demolished) George IV Hotel previously on the corner, it would have been simple. But after repeated forays by predatory highway engineers, old Edinburgh now resembled a patchwork quilt after too much washing: fabric shrunk, and the gaps between dominating the buildings rather than the reverse. The width of George IV Bridge had been extended south into Lindsay Street, compressing the museum out of sight back down Chambers Street. In response, the architects extruded a section of the 'Scotland Transformed' floor – out over the pavement like an open filing cabinet drawer – to tempt the eye from the distant Lawnmarket, and pull you along the windy avenue of blank façades and monuments that George IV Bridge has become (three churches, the National Library and Edinburgh Central Library). Halfway down, the museum's powerful tawny stone entrance tower emerges round the corner of Chambers Street.

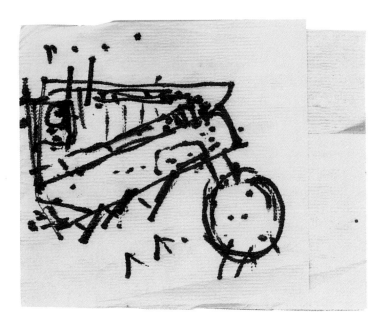
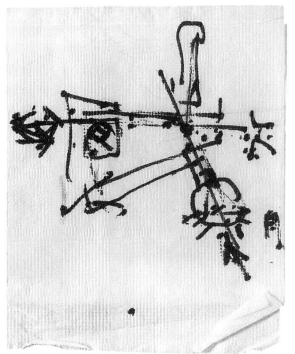

Gordon Benson's doodles
of the essence of the
competition design, on
paper napkins. The one
on the right is a diagram
of the axial views to be
had from the centre of
the design: the east end
of the Hawthornden Court.

Opposite:
Bridge crossing the
Hawthornden Court at
the east end.

## The design

By removing the Library, the Scottish Information Centre and proposed shop into the old building, the new building was liberated to focus upon Scotland. The principal reason for their success in the competition was Benson + Forsyth's decision to organise the displays in a multi-storeyed tower of reasonably flexible core galleries enveloped by a wall of potentially less flexibly-shaped study galleries. The core galleries lay to the south of the primary axis which ran from the centre of the Royal Museum's Main Hall to the east gable of Greyfriars Kirk. (The entrance from the old museum to the new has the same width as the entrance gate into Greyfriars.) The secondary axis, likewise focused upon Greyfriars, ran from the Royal Museum's entrance colonnade through a new door in the west wing wall. The triangular form of the Hawthornden Court is the result of two widely-spaced entrances becoming focused upon the same point. The junction between the Hawthornden Court and the original Royal Museum Main Hall was to be a tight, circular space in the former Hall of Power that, by compressing the link, would have enhanced the spatial explosion on either side.

In 1877 the Royal Museum's Main Hall was a teaching location, replete with viewing platforms, china stoves, pulpits, pagodas, fonts, tombs, stones, display cases and statues. It is now an enormous, glowing, largely empty antechamber to the encircling exhibitions. In total contrast the Hawthornden Court, the architects' response to the empty spaciousness of the Main Hall, was 'carved out of the solid', framed by street-high stone or plastered walls. Originally it was to be adorned with

significant icons.[20] In design and display development, the idea became fraught with difficulty, with the result that the Court remained largely empty. It takes the swelling graciousness of the Main Hall and compresses it to an apex, transforming the rational orthogonal geometry into medieval idiosyncrasy. From a rational, explicit hall, with everything visible like an enormous orangery, you pass to a space of concealed geometries and half glimpses. The Court is separated from its enclosing walls by bridges, and takes the form of a platform or a landing: an outside/inside space of stone walls, stone floor and flights of steps up and down – just as you might experience, for example, in Milne's Court off the Lawnmarket. The character of the two museum halls was intended to be different but complementary.

The far, western, end of the Hawthornden Court is the geometric pivot of the design. Straight ahead lies Greyfriars; sharp left lies the seventeenth century, and half right offers a long horizon out onto George IV Bridge. The long axis eastwards leads back to the Royal Museum Main Hall. The architects dislike over-geometricised buildings, and prefer any underlying order to be only subliminally perceived, in balance with the total experience, as it is in Charles Rennie Mackintosh's Hill House.

The core of the museum's displays is contained within the vertically-proportioned tower of galleries that rises 'like a box with openings' to one side of the Hawthornden Court. It has a surreal resemblance to a typical fifteenth-century Scottish country house: low entrance floor with cellars full of things pulled from fields, the *piano nobile* above containing the fine apartments. On the second floor (for this was a high-quality tower house) there is a 'skied gallery', a bright, dormer-window-lit gallery as can be found in Claypotts or Crathes; save that the dormer windows have become a clerestory, and it has subverted into a turbine hall with Victorian overtones. The floors above lie, as it were, 'in the thickness of the walls'. The rooftop viewing platform and parapet was to be reached by a turnpike stair. This tower was surrounded by slender top-lit light shafts running top to bottom, echoing Edinburgh closes, which detached it from the horizontally-proportioned wings of study galleries. Not only did these lightwells delineate the tower itself, they brought light right down to 'Early People' in the basement, to counteract the potential for claustrophobia and making the limestone floors feel like outdoor pathways.

A round tower squatted in the angle where the curtain wall of study galleries had been chamfered at the corner of Chambers Street. It had attracted the assessors since, as Dowson put it, it 'broke the formality of Adam and modulated down to medieval Edinburgh'.[21] At the competition stage, the tower was a storey lower and thereby squatter, much more of the proportion of Robert Adam's awesome 1777 rotunda in memory of David Hume in Calton Cemetery (itself modelled on the tomb of Theodoric in Ravenna). There was to be a detached shop on its ground floor, a chamber above reached from the interior of the museum, with a stair

Archaeologists at work on the
site at the west end of
Chambers Street in April 1991.

The Museum of Scotland tower
erupting among its neighbours.

Clashach Quarry,
Hopeman, Moray. The
striking contour markings
on the stone are clearly
visible.

At work on the building,
making shuttering.

The Chambers Street
façade, showing how it is
gradually sliced back for
the tower. *Charles McKean*

The interplay of planes
on the north wall: the
restaurant terrace at an
angle, while the window
of *The Discovery Room* is
aligned with the Royal
Museum. *Charles McKean*

Opposite:
The circular gallery on
the right now houses
*Scottish Pottery*.
Beyond it is the ghostly
Newcomen engine, and
to the left the Ellesmere
locomotive and the
whisky still – in their
protective boxes as
building continues
around them.

The west façade, with the great window of *The Reformed Church* beneath the 'filing cabinet drawer' above.
*Charles McKean*

The Museum tower from the gate into Greyfriars churchyard.
*Charles McKean*

The belvedere at the east end of the roof.

Intermediate roofscape: the white tower of the Bristo Place lift to the right. *Charles McKean*

Reflections in a tower window.

Processional doorway into the tower of the Museum of Scotland.

Opposite:
The tower of St Giles caught in the frame of the belvedere; the dome of the Bank of Scotland is to the left.

Two views from the
tower: west from the
stair and east down
Chambers Street.

Light flooding down a
turnpike stair.

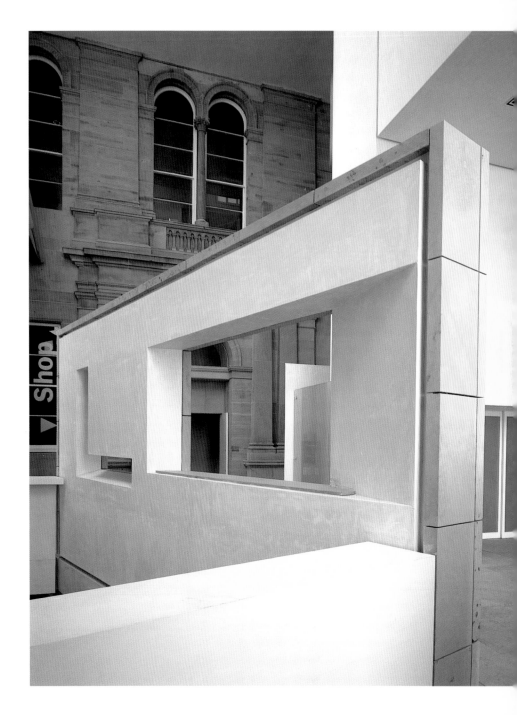

Conjunction of old and new
at ground level. The original
west façade of the Royal
Museum becomes the
eastern façade of the new
Museum.

A glimpse of light reaching the *Twentieth Century* gallery. *Charles McKean*

Architectural movement in the *Hawthornden Court*: the great flight of steps to the left, the walkway to the tower crossing the west window, and the restaurant servery billowing out high on the right. *Charles McKean*

A visor's glimpse of the
City Library and The Hub
from the Board Room.

Light shock. The brilliance
of the area linking the
Tower Restaurant to the
19th-century galleries.

The *Renaissance* gallery, looking towards *Scotland Defined* and *Na Gaidheil.*

*Trade and Industry* gallery, showing the interplay of objects in the wall cases, in standing cases, freestanding objects, and the surrounding space.

Contents of the 'turbine hall'. The power of Scotland's industrial past. On the left the cruck house from *Living on the Land*, on the right the Newcomen engine in *Power, from water to steam*.

The *Treasury of Scottish Silver*, looking out to the roof of the Newcomen engine housing.

View from the south
through to the apsidal
staircase that closes the
east end of the tower of
galleries. Beyond the
space to the right can be
glimpsed the wall of the
Royal Museum.
*Charles McKean*

Within the entrance
to *The Kingdom of
the Scots.*

curving within the wall up to a rooftop terrace rather like a broch. Round towers are powerfully symbolic. A frequent motif in Renaissance palaces, courtyards or gardens, Montaigne wrote his *Essais* in one.

The quality of light was a defining characteristic of the design. The architects warmed to the 'pristine freshness' of Scottish light: and anticipated the Hawthornden Court awash with the grey northern light. Spaces would be transformed according to the time of day and year. Rather than a static museum container, they intended a 'dynamic light-driven environment' which, in certain conditions, could produce 'light shock'. Whether freestanding or in niches, objects were always going to be more brightly illuminated than their surround,[22] and their location carefully controlled. Display cases were specified so that their frames would be concealed and 'the artefacts appeared to be within the wall structure'.[23] Complete rooms – Queen Mary's room from Rossend Castle, a Kirkcaldy merchant's room, and the great Drawing Room from Hamilton Palace – were to be visited in *culs-de-sac*, as in the Burrell Gallery. East of the core galleries lay the lighthouse collection, celebrating the triumph of man over nature with the Sule Skerry (containing the largest lens used by the Northern Lighthouse Board), Eilan Glas and Girdle Ness lanterns.

The winning design was organised around a route adorned with the icons of Scotland with accidentally disclosed vistas. It was conceived as 'an architectural promenade. Any museum should have a logical circular journey. There should be a legibility in how you experience a museum and in the sequence of its major components. Spatial hierarchy is essential to avoid endless museumitis.'[24] Curators would select their icons, and the architects add spirituality through their positioning. Any visitor turning a corner, broaching a threshold, or puffing to the top of a flight, would be experiencing a tightly controlled view. Not only did the architects intend that 'there should always be something else to see around the corner', but that how that object was encountered should contribute to your understanding of it.

Once emerged into the Hawthornden Court from the cylindrical lobby in the Royal Museum, a visitor could choose to descend to the archaeological excavations, wheel left into medieval Scotland, or ascend the great stair to the 'turbine hall'. Against the wall of the old museum was an apsidal staircase – a narrow, shallowly curving stair within thick walls 'like a broch' – gliding to the upper floors. As it rose (originally from the basement), and the windows became larger, the architecture became a metaphor for the passage of time. Escape stairs lay in the perimeter wings, and a turnpike stair rose through the principal floors of the tower's core galleries.

Compelled by the brief to appear no higher than that of the Royal Museum, the roof was the climax of the design.[25] But roof levels in Chambers Street are deceptive. The downhill slope eastwards has the result that the University's cornice is at the same level as the museum's restaurant. The roof design therefore evolved as 'a three-dimensional umbrella'. The height of most of it conforms to that of the Royal Museum, whereas – largely imperceptible from the street – the 'tower' rises behind, and the lower level of the circular tower took the scale down to that of Greyfriars. Having, as it were, pushed the boat out for the roof, the design gloried in it. Approached originally up the turnpike stair, the hanging valley concept was realised as a 'Scottish garden' adorned with a stone circle, a cluster of standing stones, much foliage, and a temple-like belvedere approached up a further flight of steps to a vista focused upon Arthur's Seat. The trees were to be Scots pine, the shrubs needle furze and gorse, with a leavening of orchids and heathland grasses.

That was it. A small number of moves in the disposition of the larger elements of the building, underpinned by a philosophy that derived design inspiration from both the objects and the city, using an architectural language that, carrying international influences, aspired to reveal inherited memory and 'remanipulate the language of the past to the present'. It was a design generated by the site rather than imposed upon it; and its architectural language of strongly modelled stone or harled geometric forms was an abstraction from it. In the extent of its absorption with its location, it was very late twentieth century.

## Construction

The construction strategy was determined by the need to get the plant off the roof, by setting the grid at a scale to accommodate the largest objects, and by managing the interrelationship between the old and new buildings. The roof was released from the normal quotidian twentieth-century roof duty of acting as a machinery platform by deep excavation, a plant sub-basement concealed beneath archaeology. By putting the building plant in the sub-basement, and taking air up through the walls themselves – 'the walls are hollow with ducts' – they avoided the need for false ceilings. The vertical space released was sufficient for the addition of two mezzanines, and these provided the opportunity for variations in spatial scale that addressed curators' concern lest the building's form overshadow preponderantly small objects. The mezzanines provided domestic, tighter, lower spaces for their display, in counterpoint to the taller hall spaces. The competition conditions made no mention of ceiling heights, presumably on the assumption that they would be constant between the two buildings.

The Museum of Scotland's structural grid was object-driven since it had to accommodate a giant waterwheel, an eighteenth-century state room, a railway engine and a pit-head beam engine – to say nothing of a portion of a cruck house. The engineer Tony Hunt recommended that the cheapest method of construction

was to provide a concrete frame to an eventual 7.5 m grid with floorslabs of 300 mm. The columns, slabs and trusses were only going to be manifest where they contributed to the story. Otherwise they were to be devoured by the fat walls.

## Chambers Street

The NMS, particularly Lord Perth, had been keen to use the new building as a catalyst for improvements to Chambers Street. It had negotiated hard with the City Council and the Highway Authority, Lothian Region (loath to lose valuable car parking places), with some

prospect of success. Between the first and second stages of the competition, the NMS had issued a supplementary note indicating that radical ideas for the future of Chambers Street would be welcome.[26] To the architects, it was as much a potential space as those they were carving within the site. 'We thought there should be exhibits in the street ... and placed standing stones in the middle, implying that the museum could extend out to it.'[27] Taking advantage of the eastward slope, they designed a pedestrianised platform extending to West College Street, floored it with a grid of setts and stone pavings, and adorned it with an avenue of plane trees, seats and statuary.

*The Workshop of the World* on Level 4 mezzanine, which provides space for large free-standing objects. On the right is the Newcomen engine. Objects in cases within the 'fat walls' can be seen on the left

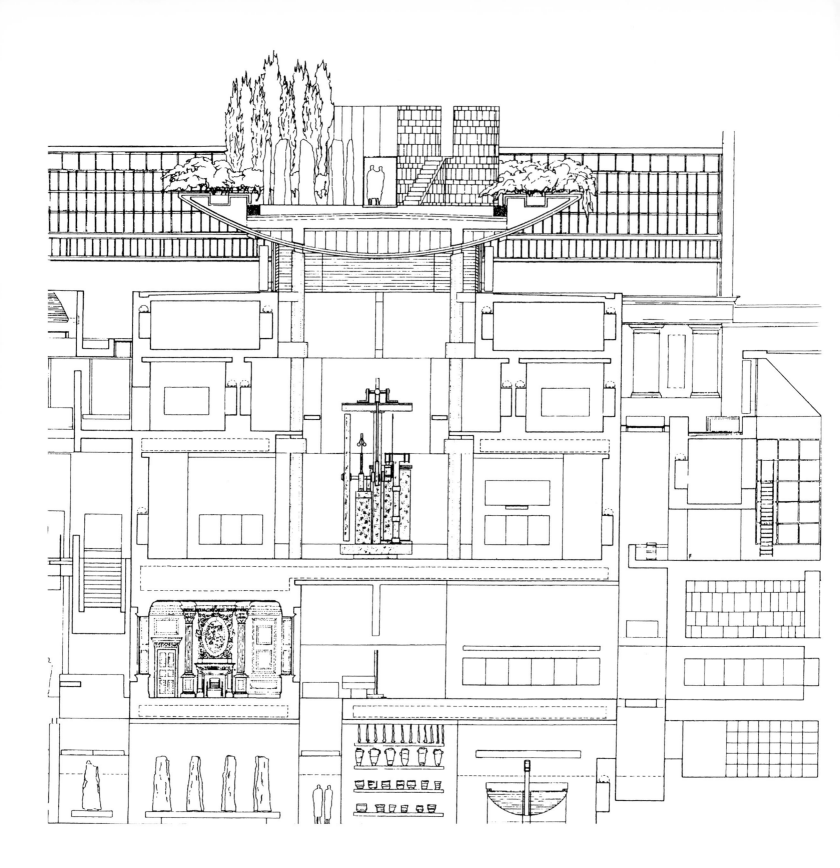

## Presentation

The assessors had been seeking a design 'that would respond to the visitor's sense of curiosity',[28] and Benson + Forsyth's presentation fitted perfectly. Seeking to convey a design that eschewed the 'air conditioned emptiness' (of, for example, the Sainsbury Centre in East Anglia University), their competition drawings were awash with symbolism and mythology in a blend of the austere and the luscious (highly appropriate to a culture of public probity and private vice). Plain, precisely calligraphed line-drawings, with every piece of dressed stone carefully outlined by hand, were juxtaposed with floating, freehand thick-lined vignettes which explained how the principal pieces of the building came together, and tempting representations of the objects: a 1960s collage rethought for the 1990s.

The axonometric revealed how the new building fed off and gave focus to the old in a relationship of mother and stepson. Perspectives of the Hawthornden Court implied a cavernous stone-lined space like a narrowing Edinburgh close, drawing the eye to a faint glimpse of Greyfriars' east façade. A view from a brilliantly lit cylindrical tower, through a tall strip window, narrow like a gunloop rising from floor to roof, gazed out into a Scottish night toward the floodlit castle. Artefacts like the waterwheel, the Hamilton Palace room, the Cockcroft Walton generator[29] and the Newcomen engine, were given iconic status. Down below, amongst 'Early Peoples', the architects had sought to convey the impression of an archaeological dig with a longboat, the Roman Bridgeness slab, the Hilton of Cadboll stone, a stone circle and avenue, serried ranks of standing stones, and shelves of pots illuminated as icons. It was the opposite of a museum consisting of circulation at the perimeter with a black box behind, about which the Trustees had been so deeply unenthusiastic in Canada.

The planners had requested a visual gap between the new building and the Royal Museum's west pavilion to mimic West College Street. The architects'

The link between the Royal Museum and the Museum of Scotland.
*Charles McKean*

The Museum of Scotland, the tower, and the east gable of Greyfriars Kirk seen from the east.
*Charles McKean*

Opposite:
Cross-section drawing looking east, showing the Newcomen engine in the centre. To the left on the level below is the Hamilton Palace room.

response was to provide a substantial glass curtain wall set-back, which could also act as a school party arrival point. The stone wall of the new museum began beyond this, with a rusticated stone pilaster in homage to the old building: but its line was then cut back at an angle, parts of the wall such as the oriel window to the Discovery Centre appearing as though they have been pulled out to conform to the original line. The widening gap thus created at the corner of Chambers Street was anchored by the circular entrance tower. The angle between the museum corner and the drum satisfied the architects' fondness for 'diminishing geometries'.[30]

The competition assessors considered that the way Benson + Forsyth had modulated between a street of large institutions lying to the east and the relics of old Edinburgh to the west was masterly.[31] They were particularly impressed by the way that the Hawthornden Court was designed to extend the vista from the wondrous galleried hall of the existing Royal Museum – one of the greatest urban rooms in Edinburgh, as Benson put it – through the new building to a window, focused axially upon the east façade of Greyfriars Kirk. They enthused about the architects' plan to extend museum activities out into a pedestrianised Chambers Street:[32] an ambition not yet relinquished.[33]

The drum tower was aligned not with the Royal Museum's pavilions but with their projecting cornice. It thus appears to advance slightly, giving Chambers Street a sense of termination that it has hitherto lacked. It was depicted with a roof terrace, vegetation hanging over and concealing the edge, so that in elevation it resembled a romantic crumbling ruin against the Castle backdrop. Wordsworth, Coleridge, and William Beckford would have taken the point. The assessors certainly did. '*The winning design was synoptic of Scottish culture and its material artefacts.*'[34] The designers hoped, simply, to create a building that could mature.

# Notes

1 Benson + Forsyth notes, 13.7.1999.

2 Interview with Gordon Benson. The majority of information, and all the unattributed or unreferenced quotations, come from interviews with Gordon Benson and/or the design team at interviews listed in 'Sources'.

3 Gordon Benson, quoted in Hugh Pearman: *Sunday Times* 18.8.1991.

4 Interview with Gordon Benson.

5 Benson + Forsyth notes 13.7.1999.

6 Benson + Forsyth subsequently won the (abortive) competition to extend Edinburgh Central Library on a site which rose from the Cowgate valley many floors up to the early nineteenth-century levels of George IV Bridge.

7 Interview with Gordon Benson.

8 Benson + Forsyth notes 13.7.1999.

9 Interview with Sir Philip Dowson.

10 Interview with Dr Robert Anderson.

11 Benson + Forsyth notes 13.7.1999.

12 The Burrell Gallery has *circa* 4900 m² of display space, and the MoS *circa* 7000 m².

13 A tower of seven floors was well within the vertiginous urban traditions of Edinburgh.

14 Interview with Gordon Benson.

15 The roof was released from mechanical drudgery by removing the mechanical plant to deep excavations.

16 My emphasis. It implies that in the architects' perception, the museum experience would have been incomplete without them.

17 Benson + Forsyth notes 13.7.1999.

18 'It is proposed that ... areas of solid walling are metal panels, probably pressed panels of matt (heavily shot-blasted) stainless steel, which will weather to a soft, uniform silver-grey colour'. Richards: 'Feasibility', p 23.

19 1892 paper on 'Architecture' in Pamela Robertson (ed): *Charles Rennie Mackintosh – the Architectural Papers*, p 186.

20 Shown on the competition drawings.

21 Interview with Sir Philip Dowson.

22 Script on the competition-winning drawings.

23 Interview with Gordon Benson.

24 Ibid.

25 A proposal to begin the building's journey at roof level in the midst of prehistory had separately and simultaneously enticed the curators. Amongst the many advantages was that modern objects were likely to be larger and more easily accommodated at ground level. Dr Robert Anderson dished the notion as too complicated.

26 Presentation made to MoS Client Committee 17.11.1995. Information from Ian Hooper.

27 Interview with Gordon Benson.

28 Interview with Philip Dowson 2.6.1998.

29 A 1951 descendant from that which had split the atom, symbolic of High Tech Science, it finally failed to secure a place in the new building.

30 Interview with Gordon Benson.

31 Interview with Sir Philip Dowson 2.6.1998.

32 Interview with Lord Perth.

33 Letter from Lord Perth to Mark Jones 10.7.1999.

34 Interview with Sir Philip Dowson 2.6.1998.

# Gearing up

Immediately following the competition press conference, Bute hosted a house party at Mount Stuart for the architects, Robert Anderson, Peter Jones, Ian Hooper and their families. Nowadays it might be characterised as a bonding session, with a relaxed atmosphere with good food and excellent wines. Serious matters were left to Sunday: the practicality and relevance of the proposed roof garden; the junction between old and new museums; the necessity to rationalise and simplify both the complexity of the interlocking ideas and of the details; and the extent to which the design depended upon using space within the Royal Museum building for its success.[1] Bute's purpose was to develop mutual respect, and to test the type of collaboration he envisaged. The architects were already fearful lest their design be watered down or undermined as people tried 'to take everything away from us' during the development process. Bute gave Benson + Forsyth the undertaking that 'if you convince me intellectually, I will give you my full support'. What struck them was his 'passion for the enterprise on behalf of Scotland'.[2]

The completion of the competition signalled the end of the initiation phase of the Museum of Scotland. It was now a matter of delivering the largest project the NMS had ever undertaken, involving both risk and fundraising. Appropriate experience was added to the Trustees with Alistair (later Sir Alistair) Grant and the Countess of Dalkeith, whose first meeting comprised a somewhat lordly presentation of the winning scheme as a *fait accompli*,[3] accompanied by a video of the Boarbank Oratory as an example of the architects' approach to detail.[4] Trustees like Grant, Chairman of the Argyll Group, and Deputy Chairman Robert Smith, a banker, were intended to carry credibility with a government obsessed with the private sector, if they decided to select any commissioning or contracting procedures that deviated from the norm.[5]

Most inconveniently, Robert Anderson had been appointed Director of the British Museum some months earlier. Having achieved a successful design against such odds, the Trustees were not minded to cast doubt upon it. So Anderson's successor had to be somebody who, by and large, accepted the winning design. Six months later, in January 1992, Mark Jones arrived from the British Museum as Director. Ian Hooper's responsibilities as Project Director were extended to cover all aspects of building delivery – budget, content, contracts, consultant appointment and exhibition development. All communication between NMS staff and the architects was to pass through him – with the Trustees imposing the contradictory and unrealisable

> **" Just what is a museum or gallery supposed to do or look like these days? This is a trick question. The answer is: it does not matter. The only important thing is that it should be designed by a world-famous architect. The building (the medium) is becoming more important than the content (the message) .... The Sainsbury wing, the Sainsbury Centre, St Ives, Pompidou, Clore Gallery ... the Pompidou effects or the Guggenheim effects. What is in the museum? Who cares? Ride the lifts, gasp at the views, eat the food, go home. It is time we owned up to the fact that all these fine architects are designing adult playpens. "**
>
> *Hugh Pearman*
> Sunday Times, *12 May 1991.*

Opposite:
The building goes up.
*Niall Hendrie*

89

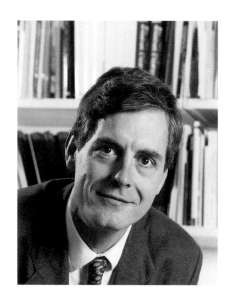

Mark Jones became
Director of the National
Museums of Scotland
in 1992.

caveat that nothing should reduce 'the importance of dialogue between the architects and curatorial staff in the development of the designs for the exhibition areas'.[6]

That autumn occurred Bute's first absence for what was eventually to prove a terminal illness (leading to Robert Smith becoming Chairman of Trustees in 1993).

## Spatial rethink

Upon appointment, Jones re-appraised the NMS accommodation to conclude that 'divided locations [were] bad for staff morale and efficiency'.[7] Port Edgar was environmentally inadequate, insecure and inaccessible, and Leith Customs House unsatisfactory and overcrowded. He recommended immediate action to unite staff, renew permanent galleries, and replace premises – ideally on a single site. Since that was unattainable in Chambers Street, he proposed a twin-site strategy: a more intensive development at Chambers Street, with the site at West Granton as the principal location for collections, storage, associated laboratories and workshops. It would also provide facilities for research and conservation.[8]

How much more space could Chambers Street provide? Visitor surveys indicated that the ground floor galleries attracted twice as many visitors as those on the first, and three times as many as those in the second,[9] implying that the upper floors of lesser-used galleries might be a good place to begin. Although Hall 22, lying against the south-west corner, had been destined for continued use by the Library, with an Information Centre, Benson suggested new floors in the air space above.[10] So (underestimating the strength of its structure) Hall 22 was to be demolished behind its façade to provide three floors of offices above two floors of galleries.[11] The enfolding redevelopment of Hall 22 improved the circulation of the museum beyond compare. Clearer east-west interconnections were created through the Byzantine labyrinths of the invisible south side of the Royal Museum, partly beside and partly above a large immured stump of Edinburgh's Flodden Wall. A new staff entrance from Bristo Port was conveniently adjacent to the NMS's new delivery bays. Crucially, once Hall 22 was complete, museum staff could finally quit the former NMAS buildings in Queen Street and unite with their colleagues. Construction began eventually in July 1994 and over the following two years provided the customary distractions of inner city building – complaints about noise and dust, and (once foundations were begun for the new museum) allegations of cracking in neighbouring properties.[12] The project had the additional value of acting as a test-bed for Benson + Forsyth's architecture, components and details.

The competition design had also proposed the use of Hall 21 for the expanded Library. The new Director was unconvinced that another substantial, publicly accessible Library was needed so close to the National Library of Scotland, barely

100 yards away. In any case, the NMS needed the gallery space. So the existing Library remained *in situ*, with extensive new stacking added to the basement to cope with the arrivals from the Society of Antiquaries of Scotland's Library in Queen Street.

## Money and politics

Robert Smith's acceptance of Malcolm Rifkind's challenge in 1987 to raise private sector funding for the fitting out had led to the establishment of the Patrons' organisation. Bute took the view that the Trustees had committed themselves only to raising £5 million towards the cost of fitting-out, whereas the government decided to hold the Trustees responsible for raising funds for everything except the construction.[13] No one was clear where the building funded by the government stopped, and where fitting-out began. £5 million soon emerged as a significant underestimate. In 1992, at a time when the NMS was seeking approval from the Scottish Office to proceed to detailed design, Hooper informed the Trustees that, making comparisons with similar institutions, fitting-out could cost as much as £20 million. It was unwelcome news, so by the following meeting he had reduced it by making significant cuts to the specification to £10-12 million. At a difficult meeting between the Trustees and the fundraising committee, Lord Perth stated its reluctance to contemplate a target higher than £7 million. Further cuts, down to a 'radically economic specification', proved unworkable.[14]

The opening fundraising event for the new museum was, in homage to its successor, a gala dinner and auction hosted by the Society of Antiquaries of Scotland.[15] But fundraising had to change gear. Outside fundraisers were rejected since they would not be able to tap into the museum's own networks so easily, and a campaign director was appointed from within in 1993.[16] Now the benefit of the Patrons became evident. Several of them were old friends of Bute or Perth, but many complete strangers responded to letters of invitation to become patrons with astounding enthusiasm.[17] Perth remained Chairman of the organisation, and the Countess of Dalkeith became the Trustee particularly associated with the appeal (later succeeding Perth as Chairman). The appeal was directed at those with Scottish roots, and the American appeal was launched with a fundraising event on the royal yacht 'Britannia' in February 1994. International fundraising depended for its success upon having an effective local presence, which accounts for the success of the American appeal (where there was) and the lack of success in Australia and Hong Kong (where there was not).[18]

Fundraising proved easier for particular projects. The Discovery Centre, for example, was funded by the Lloyds TSB Foundation and the Esmée Fairbairn Trust; the Hawthornden Court by Mrs H J Heinz and named after her Midlothian seat (Drummond of Hawthornden's); and the diminutive cinema in the Twentieth

The emergence of the new administration offices on the site of Hall 22 to the rear of the Royal Museum.

Her Majesty the Queen inspects the model of the new building at the launch of the fundraising campaign, July 1994.

Century gallery by the Post Office.[19] Many Scottish banks and businesses responded generously 'because it was Scotland and its history'.[20] Expectations for the new building and its contents were heightened in thousands of appeal letters dispatched to the Scots diaspora. Yet as the appeal income rose, so did the likely costs always overleap it. By 1994 the amount pledged had reached almost £4 million but the target cost had risen to £14.5 million.[21] Closing the gap was going to be impossible by fundraising alone. An application for matching funding – 'a proxy for the entire idea'[22] – was accordingly made to the Heritage Lottery Fund, and its success added £7.25 million to the fitting-out fund. It was one of the first such applications, and Perth attributed the good fortune of NMS to its prior success in international fundraising. 'Raising our own money gave us a sense of freedom, and earned the respect of the Scottish Office.'[23] Lord Rothschild, then Chairman of the Lottery Fund, expressed his delight at being able to assist 'one of the great, great projects of the last decade of the 20th century … a huge project, brilliantly put together and thought through'.[24] By June 1998 income raised as a result of that pledge given to the government back in 1987 had reached £8.5 million which, added to the Lottery funding, covered a total fitting-out cost not far out of line with Hooper's 1992 prediction.

Yet even fundraising success on this scale provided no exemption from political revisionism. Scottish Office ministers changed; and the new Secretary of State, Michael Forsyth, had no loyalty to the project. Wise to the risk of cancellation, the NMS had been canny in undertaking the pre-emptive excavation of the foundations, consolidation works, and works to Hall 22. With so much already invested, the argument went, it would be poor husbanding of public funds not to proceed. Yet even such a large concrete-lined hole in the ground proved little protection against a political predator, and in 1995 the NMS got wind that the project was again at risk. The Chairman, Robert Smith, and the Director made ready to face out the Scottish Office, arguing that everything was too far committed to stop. Indeed, if the project were cancelled, all Trustees would resign.[25] Forsyth's civil servants advised him that 'the train had already left the station', and Smith and Jones were duly summoned in autumn 1995 to learn the Secretary of State's decision at a formal meeting. The project could continue. Their bland report to the Trustees of 'a useful meeting'[26] concealed moments of high anxiety.

### The changing nature of museums

Museums, like architects, are always good for a grin at a cocktail party. The Museum of Scotland was emerging at a time when so many new museums, art galleries and heritage centres were being constructed that their civic and educational purposes, their presentation, interpretation and display techniques were all being re-appraised. So, just when its building design was beginning to harden – and the idea of 'Scotland' was remaining obstinately fluid – old certainties about museums were dissolving. Why did governments fund them and what services were they expected to provide? If, as some local authorities believed, visitor numbers were now to be used as the measure of success, would that not be incompatible with research and scholarship?

In the first annual A W Franks lecture in 1997, Sir Nicholas Goodison suggested that a museum's overriding duty must be to maintain its collections.[27] As an educational institution 'which inspired those who were receptive to inspiration', it served the public best by recording, conserving, displaying and explaining its objects to visitors. Objects should not be used in interpretative tableaux in such a way that they could not be appreciated for themselves. Nor should they be reduced to the level of amusement. 'Works of art and other objects defy such abuse …. They speak for the ages in which they were made, and of the artists and craftsmen who made them.'[28] On the other hand, the number of museum visits had multiplied by three times in the last three decades, and visitors had expectations of attractive displays, stimulating interpretation, good food, a well-stocked shop and access for the disabled.[29]

The primary function of the Museum of Scotland building was to be that of a display and interpretation centre of, primarily, Scottish objects. The collecting, curating, conservation, storage and research activities of a normal museum would be carried on off-site, mainly in the Royal Museum and the new Granton Centre. Since the Williams' Committee had placed education as a principal objective, NMS curators had in the intervening period become much more open to the idea that visitors would put their own interpretation on objects. The chronological, national narrative (see 'Exhibition evolution', page 101) implied a comprehensive collection. This the NMS did not fully possess, but it would be complemented by material in other locations. So the narrative implied that the museum's displays would, as relevant, signpost visitors to other collections where they could discover more. The Trustees were enthusiastic. 'Since it could not tell all of Scotland's story, it should therefore point visitors towards the huge potential resource in the 300 or so local museums in Scotland.'[30] The NMS held regional seminars during 1992-3 to examine how such interaction might be developed.

A seminar was held in 1993 to re-assess best practice in interpretation techniques, focused upon 'communication through display'. Emerging general principles were then formalised into exhibition guidelines.[31] There should be, above all, in Robert Louis Stevenson's words, 'a strong Scotch accent of the mind'. The guidelines stated: 'Our presentation, language and tone should all contribute to conveying the material and cultural environment of Scotland and Scots. Someone helicoptered blindfold into the Museum of Scotland should at once have a sense

*Niall Hendrie*

Queen Mary's harp displayed in a context that highlights the disparate origins of the peoples of Scotland.

of where he is.'[32] Other guidelines were physical: 'There must be opportunities for seating'; some linguistic: 'The majority of gallery titles should be in clear plain English'; and others visual: 'Graphic panels outside the cases must be consistent with the overall architectural and exhibition design.'

Visitors were graded according to likely knowledge and interest – from the 'baby browser' up to the 'specialist'. The guidelines required that 'at least 80% of the messages should be understandable to at least 80% of the visitors; and that 50% of the displays should be capable of being understood by upper primary school pupils'.[33] The difficulties lay in forecasting the extent of the visitors' prior knowledge, and how to identify messages that the visitors might not spot without assistance from captions. Mock-ups of proposed displays – entire areas with all their proposed spatial, lighting and graphic characteristics, accompanied by fact sheets on various themes – were prepared as 'testbed projects' for submission to audience reaction. They sought, particularly, to evaluate visitor reaction to content, layout, presentation, 'hands-on' opportunities, graphics, lighting, and colour. The research was to examine whether the messages of the displays had been communicated adequately.[34] Responses were typically diverse: some seeking more information, others admitting that they never read labels. The testbed on mediaeval churches brought the obvious 'in Canada, we don't have any medieval churches'.[35] Overseas tourists were uncomfortable touching precious objects since they felt that it would only damage them.[36]

The research led to changes to sequence method and graphics: shorter text, in a different colour, improved legibility at wheelchair level, and significant textual revision, so that the contents were conveyed with greater clarity (how important were the bishops?). Testbeds were then submitted for a second review. *Pace* the Whig theory of history, not every change was an improvement, and the original proposals were sometimes deemed better. The most important testbed result, however, was that visitors found the displays generally old-fashioned for the late twentieth century. They wanted more sophisticated presentation techniques, with more hands-on experience, more interactive exhibits, and more to interest young people. The successful use of audio in the testbed on coal stimulated the development of the portable sound guide with its music and sound effects.[37]

The NMS educational strategy thereafter, advised by a Teachers' Development Group, focused upon how schools could be encouraged to use the new museum. Objects contained cultural information of a value equal to that of textbooks, and it wanted to show how object-based learning could offer a valuable addition to education. One project was 'fifty questions you can ask of an object'.[38] A Junior Board to give a child's perspective, consisting of twelve children aged between nine and fourteen selected from schools from around the country, was sponsored by Scottish Enterprise. An early visit was to the coal testbed. The NMS was chastened to learn

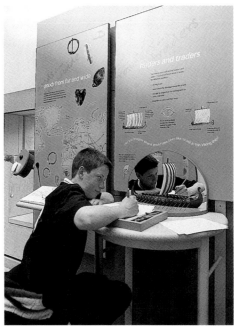

where the proposed approach was hard to comprehend, and pleased where it conveyed the idea immediately.[39] The Junior Board, in turn, found some of its ideas impractical, whereas others would influence the final displays. Board Members helped identify and select objects with special interest for children, and wrote labels for fifty of them. One, comparing a CD player to an old His Master's Voice 78 rpm gramophone record player, concluded, 'but what's a record?'

Although hands-on interactive exhibitions, flip books, and objects on shelves projecting from the walls, emerged as the favourite type of display, the fragility of many of the objects, and the design of the cases, limited such opportunities.[40] The educational approach throughout the museum was therefore text based, enhanced by the 'discovery points' and interactive screen presentations. Only in the Discovery Centre, on the first floor overlooking Chambers Street,

were the interactive aspirations of the Teachers' Development Group and the Junior Board fully realised. The Centre, a late arrival funded by the appeal (emphasising the connection between the appeal and the project's development), encourages formal school groups or informal browsers to touch and consider replicas or objects from the handling collections. The experience is designed both to be fun – an approach continued in the children's guide *On the Trail of Scotland's Past* – and to satisfy the object-based learning objectives of the school curriculum.

Market research established a profile of likely visitors, gauged their reactions to the concept of the Museum of Scotland, and assessed the proposed museum facilities.[41] Visitors were emphatic that the museum display should be organised chronologically rather than by subject, desired interactive displays, and welcomed the idea of computers and video – provided they did not have to queue to use them.

Existing museums were criticised for poor, overpriced food and having nowhere to sit.[42] So long as it was not done tackily, most appeared content if attendants were clad in tartan – with the exception of visitors from Newcastle, who preferred young, informal helpers in jeans and sweatshirts. Displays were therefore reviewed for 'appropriate use of material for chronological orientation', and captions rewritten with shorter sentences, key points highlighted, enlivened by bullet points distinguishing each aspect of the object. The visitor was to be taken 'from the familiar to the unfamiliar' and the information 'seasoned with fun'.

## New technologies

From the project's inception in 1986 the NMS had been keen to use the new technologies to communicate the museum's treasures to a wider audience. A pre-emptive suggestion of an archaeological computer game called GROPE (Games Review of Prehistoric Evidence) may have been rather advanced for 1987,[43] but the original Museum of Scotland concept included an Information Centre for Scottish Culture, based on the NMS computer system. Given Trustee enthusiasm, the next step for the emerging multimedia group[44] was to demonstrate what new types of access could be achieved using the new technology. The sum of £50,000 per annum for three years was made available for trials of remote access and the development of multimedia; in parallel to the huge task of creating a database of the NMS collections.[45]

Public use of information technology became focused upon MOSAICS[46] and SCRAN.[47] A joint venture by the NMS, the Royal Commission on the Ancient and Historical Monuments of Scotland and the Scottish Museums Council, SCRAN was the first and only large Information Technology partnership project to be supported by the Millennium Commission, being granted £7.5 million in 1996. It developed the vision of the Museum of Scotland as a synoptic introduction to the extraordinary wealth of material in collections elsewhere, through providing an illustrated database of objects from the Museum of Scotland and many other collections. Reducing the problem of geographic distance, it is accessed through computers and enjoyed throughout the country.

Multimedia was an expensive way of interpreting an object (most of the cost lying not in the hardware but in making the programmes); and where objects could be interpreted more cheaply in traditional ways, that would be the chosen option. The team of researchers, graphic designers and programmers forming the multimedia group developed brief interactive presentations on objects that could not be examined in such detail. The presentations bring noise and the music to the experience that is otherwise lacking in the museum (except through a sound guide): the Newcomen engine huffs and puffs into life; and it might give even the most blasé

visitor a disconcerting moment when encouraged to touch-activate the Maiden (the sixteenth-century decapitating device) and hear the sound and thump as it rushes down to its victim. The screen presentation of whisky-making alongside the whisky-still explains how the latter worked. The most remarkable result is the way that small precious objects, which could never be handled by the public, have been gloriously and colourfully brought larger than life. By touching the screen, enlarging, reducing or rotating an object like the golden Hunterston Brooch or an ivory-pale Lewis chessman, you can study detail, carving or inscription that would otherwise be impossible. The programme can demonstrate what damaged objects would have looked like originally by replacing missing bits.

IT has become central to the Museum of Scotland experience. Multimedia 'articles' or computer essays on the 'large and recalcitrant issues' underlying the principal displays which the latter were unable to develop in adequate depth, can be studied in the ExhibIT room, in the south-east corner of the ground floor.[48] Recollections of donors can be overheard in the Memory Bank in the Twentieth Century gallery. Twenty-odd monitors throughout the galleries examine the background to an object, and show it recreated in use, thus helping communicate context and any underlying themes. IT has solved, very neatly, the conflict between the need to conserve objects and the need to provide greater access to them.

## Conservation

The creation of the new museum required the identification and selection of, originally, some 12,500 objects, then making an assessment of their condition prior to preparing approximately 10,000 for display. For conservation purposes, they were classified from those that required no conservation treatment at all to those on the verge of dissolution.[49] The Newcomen engine arrived as a collection of huge bits, including its three-ton six-metre beam. Having been conserved at Granton, it required re-assembling at the same time as the engine house was built to support it. The boiler cladding of the Ellesmere locomotive was wholly rusted and its chimney was missing. The conservators had to return it to 'just refurbished' order, which involved the re-making of certain parts. During the process, they discovered that the engine had been modified since it had been first built – made narrower so that it could pass through tunnels. The locomotive, once repaired, was indeed intended to move and appropriate power was laid on;[50] but there proved to be insufficient space in the museum for it to do so, and the necessary health and safety guard-rails were deemed too intrusive.[51]

Ancient stones required consolidation and sometimes non-intrusive laser cleaning, in which the laser beam hits the surface, causes rapid thermal expansion, and detaches the soot. The procedure could address a spot as little as 2 mm in

Weighing a section of waterlogged wooden canoe before loading it into the freeze drier at West Granton.

diameter.[52] Incomplete, freestanding stones that had lost their original underground portion required a new type of plinth to avoid important carvings being obscured by stands (as had been the case in Queen Street). In the conservation premises in Granton, the team made precise resin moulds so that glass bases could be cast to fit the base of each differently sized stone perfectly: the stone being maintained in place by a steel tensioned rod joining stone through plinth to floor.

Conservation work for the museum stimulated much new research. The watermark on a prize Bonnie Prince Charlie letter transpired to be puzzlingly nineteenth-century. Research, which required tracking dyes worldwide, into the 1806-20 Tartan Book amassed by the Highland Society of London (long before George IV's pink trews and the post-1822 tartan-transmogrification) revealed how many of the colours had depended upon exotic dyes, including cochineal, imported from South America and the Mediterranean. It implies that, contrary to mythology, tartan more likely may have been worn as a high-status fashion accessory rather than the primitive garb of subsistence-level peasantry.[53]

The King's Colours, present at Culloden, required unpicking from 1930s conservation work, and sandwiching between two new layers of strategically dyed net. Work only thirty years old sometimes had to be unpicked. The weight of some flags required improved support, and new material was inserted behind the fabric to support weak and damaged areas. Eleven flags and banners were selected for display, but in rotation to avoid overexposure to light.

Once conserved, objects were stacked in the lower floors of Hall 22, waiting final placement.

## Notes

1 Interviews with Ian Hooper and Gordon Benson. Assessors' requirements laid out in the Report to the Board of Trustees from Sir Philip Dowson 8.8.1991, NMS (91) 4.

2 Interview with Gordon Benson 2.6.1998.

3 Interview with Sir Alistair Grant.

4 NMS Trustees Minutes 23.8.1991.

5 Interview with Ian Hooper.

6 MoSCC 93/10: 'All formal communications and instructions for NMS will be channelled through the NMS Project Director as the client's sole representative' 24.6.1993.

7 Mark Jones: 'NMS Accommodation Strategy' 10.6.1992.

8 NMS Corporate Plan 1994-8, p 4. The Granton Centre was opened by the Minister for the Arts 26.4.1996.

9 Mark Jones: 'NMS Accommodation Strategy'.

10 MoSCC 24.1.1992.

11 To be used initially for storing artefacts in the interval between conservation and installation in the new museum.

12 MoSCC 23.3.1995.

13 Information from Ian Hooper.

14 Ibid.

15 Letter from Dr Anna Ritchie 27.6.1999.

16 The NMS Head of Public Affairs, Dr Sheila Brock.

17 Interview with Lord Perth.

18 Interview with Dr Sheila Brock.

19 Ibid, on condition that it showed some films from the Post Office Film Archive.

20 Letter from Lord Perth 10.7.1999.

21 NMS Trustees minutes 11.3.1994.

22 Interview with Sir Alistair Grant.

23 Interview with Dr Sheila Brock.

24 Prospect (MoS Campaign newsletter), no 5, Winter 1993.

25 Interview with Sir Robert Smith.

26 NMS Trustees minutes 6.10.1995.

27 Goodison: A new era for Museums, p 9.

28 Ibid, p 16.

29 Ibid.

30 Ronnie Cramond to the Trustees, NMS Trustees minutes 1.3.1991.

31 By Mary Bryden and Jenni Calder.

32 Museum of Scotland – Exhibition Guidelines 1.2.1996.

33 Ibid.

34 Interview with Susan Mitchell.

35 'The mediaeval church Scotinform Test Bed Project III': Focus Group interim and final reports 5.9.1996, p 5.

36 Ibid, p 12.

37 Information from Mary Bryden.

38 Interview with Mary Bryden.

39 Ibid.

40 Interview with Susan Mitchell.

41 'Museum of Scotland Research Report', Market Research Scotland Ltd, April 1997.

42 Ibid, para 3.3.6.

43 Dr David Clarke, NBWG, part 2, 16.2.1987.

44 Led by archaeologist Dr Mike Spearman.

45 Interview with Dr Mike Spearman.

46 Museum of Scotland Advanced Interactive Computer Systems.

47 Scottish Cultural Resources Access Network (SCRAN).

48 Where visitors can also access SCRAN.

49 Interview with Dr Jim Tate.

50 Phase 1 Report, October 1995, p 16 states: 'The locomotive would require three-phase power to operate its drive machinery'– implying that movement was being contemplated.

51 Interview with Dr Allen Simpson.

52 Interview with Dr Jim Tate.

53 Interview with Hugh Cheape.

# Exhibition evolution

The purpose of the Museum of Scotland was to display things Scottish, and the public had come to expect that it would represent Scotland's culture. It had long been decided that displays should be multi-disciplinary, with objects grouped in period rather than in 'discipline dominated arrangements'.[1] Exhibition theme development, begun in 1986, was formalised by an Exhibition sub-committee co-ordinated by Jenni Calder. 'In period' implied a narrative chronological structure for the displays, which she welcomed since it offered the best opportunity of challenging myths about Scotland's past. 'Visitors, be they from Scotland or from other countries, almost certainly arrive with preconceptions about Scotland and the Scots. Though powerful, these myths are comparatively few in number and have tended to impoverish perceptions of Scottish culture.'[2] If visitors could see a lodging house booth, a bothy, a croft and perhaps a twentieth-century council house, they might be stimulated by material with which they were already familiar.[3] Seeing a concentration of Scottish objects that could be found nowhere else would force them to review their own perceptions of Scotland and of Scottish national identity. 'Where else would you find anything about the colour and aesthetics of the Reformed Church?'[4] Moreover, the NMS was keen to demonstrate how collections, previously underplayed by academic history, could be used as a valuable source of historical knowledge.

Naturally, the curators had their own aspirations for the portrayal of Scots. The Research Director wanted to convey the strange sense of sophistication emanating from ancient artefacts, indicating that Scotland in the Dark Ages 'was not overrun by barbarian hordes and, in contrast, made unique contributions to the cultural history of Europe in the period. It is clear that basic skills were not lost'.[5] The Keeper of Archaeology concurred: 'People in prehistoric and early historic times are not to be regarded as squat grunting savages leading squalid brutish lives.' He was sceptical, however, about the value of constricting archaeology within a national history: 'For 90%, in terms of time, of the human occupation of the geographical area of Scotland, the concept of a Scottish nation, as we now understand it, is meaningless; and our view of Scotland as a relatively impoverished country at the extreme edge of Europe is merely a modern map projection that provides no universal template for understanding pre-history and early history.'[6]

Nonetheless, order and context had to be given to a heterogeneous collection of 20,000 potential exhibits, over 200 of them large and uncased. They varied in scale

> **" Britain has a poor record for temperate, reasoned, public discourse about matters of taste and intellect. Perhaps we can help to remedy that situation during the years ahead in which we bring our new museum into existence. "**
>
> *Professor Peter Jones*

Opposite:
The *Ellesmere* locomotive being lowered into position in summer 1996, during construction. There would be no openings large enough once the building was complete.
*Niall Hendrie*

The reconstructed room of a Kirkcaldy merchant in the 17th century.

from roof bosses, crosses and endless timber panels to spinning machines, power looms, X-ray machines, 'Robot Freddie', a diorama, gaming machine, the Albion travelling shop, and a saurian footprint. Displays organised chronologically might well provide the visitor with the most understandable context for objects otherwise difficult to explain, but would they, in turn, be able to support a comprehensive narrative of national history? There was no necessary reason why they should. The museum's collections had grown as much by serendipity and happenchance – the accidental detritus of history – as by systematic collection. Even where there had been a rigorous programme – for example, of collecting items of technological revolution since it was believed to be in the country's interests to learn from them[7] – the objects were likely to reflect the preoccupations of the time or the passing interest of individuals. 'There is no Olympian objectivity about how a collection has been made up.'[8] There had been substantial post-war collecting ('we collected everything'[9]), but only according to the perceived objectives of the two museums at the time. Indeed, had a Museum of Scotland then existed, it might have cast its net wider – to pick up, for example, the wealth of buildings and fittings that became available during the post-war destruction of Scotland's cities and country houses. As compared to the museums of buildings and architecture abroad, the Museum of Scotland's equivalent collection remains fragmentary.

Now that it was agreed that the museum would represent the nation's culture, the NMS came under pressure to 'answer public expectations by covering, for example, the Clearances and immigration, the growth of Glasgow, and the importance of Edinburgh in the Scottish Enlightenment'.[10] But how could displays of objects communicate the passage of ideas such as the Enlightenment? Even had a pickled Enlightenment brain been available, how would it be displayed and what could it communicate? The 'A Hot Bed of Genius' exhibition attempted to portray it through the application of ideas to medicine and science, with an accompanying display of books and manuscripts. Reviewing it retrospectively, Anderson had this to say:

> A good deal of thought has, on occasion, been put into how to present an historical account by means of exhibited objects .... The ambition of the exhibition was to tell the story of the Scottish Enlightenment in a popular way .... But the process of development of the exhibition was somewhat agonising .... Clearly there are going to be problems in an exhibition on this theme central to Scottish history: how does one present Hume's views on causation, Smith's economic theory, or even Black's work on latent heat? The exhibition itself developed as a series of portraits, memorabilia and personalia backed up by the books which dealt with these intangible matters. It was an excellent experience, but, again, the well-prepared scholar would derive considerably more from it than the curious but uninformed member of the public.[11]

A SCOT

If curators were sceptical about the extent to which a chronological national narrative could be supported by the collections, they were very uncertain as to how 'national' was to be defined. Made in Scotland, made by Scots, bought for Scotland, used in Scotland, or seized for Scotland? They fretted lest displays might be tempted to stray from strict presentation and interpretation of the objects: 'The difference between a Heritage Centre and a Museum is that the latter does not attempt to make bricks without straw.'[12] The original proposal for 'Modern Times', for example, was dismissed as an unsorted collection of unconvincing items unable to sustain the weight of its story. 'Keir Hardie's silver tea service, the only significant item for the period, seems unlikely to give a representative picture of radical politics in the twentieth century.'[13] Anderson was emphatic that the selection should be based upon whatever history might emerge from the objects, rather than selecting them to illustrate received history. 'The object should tell the story, not that we should present a story illustrated by objects .... The objects should speak for themselves, and should occupy the primary role in all displays. We cannot hope for a balance, as a historian may attempt to achieve in a book .... Pure concepts cannot be directly associated with material culture.'[14] At the exhibition brief seminar, Don Aldridge had chaffed those seeking total objectivity: 'Selecting themes is helpful, because the person who knows the collection best and does the selecting is enabling the visitor to see the inter-relationships and the links .... A museum curator's job is to do this selection for me, the visitor. He is welcome to his opinion.

If some wet educational psychologist tells me that all this is elitist, I would have him visit your taxidermist.'[15]

The accidental nature of survival and collection meant that there were other gaps: very little on post-Reformation Catholicism; only a certain amount of heavy engineering; very little of significance on Clyde shipbuilding (since that had been encouraged to go to Glasgow);[16] and only a few items of furniture by those re-nowned for furniture design – Robert Adam, Charles Rennie Mackintosh and Sir Robert Lorimer. 'This apparent weakness we have sought to turn into a benefit. We have quite deliberately constructed our presentations around the idea that much of the evidence is available elsewhere in Scotland .... Our hope is that the MoS will create in visitors the wish to explore more.'[17]

Visitors' understanding would be improved by presenting the objects within coherent time bands and a recognisable context. 'Objects are direct material evidence of the past, but also something more. They have the virtue of being real things, the wood of the true cross of history. But they do not perform miracles, such as speaking for themselves. The interpretation must draw out the sense of the different worlds they belong to .... Assertions that are out of kilter with informed historical perception will get the rough passage that they deserve .... If, by some absurd alchemy, we could parade some "typical" Scotsmen from each century, we would find that they were largely foreigners to one another. Displays should avoid the sense of the past inevitably leading to the present, because that is the fodder of myth. History is full of blind alleys and unexpected breaks, and that is what makes it exciting.'[18] The trouble was that a narrative structure implied sequence, and any display based upon the accretion of knowledge in a certain order would be vulner-able to the thrawn visitor who, human and contrary, enters at the wrong end of a sequence; or, worse, grazes at random. Even where the signage is powerful, visitors will not necessarily follow direction if there is a multiplicity of choices. Could a didactic, sequential narrative cheerfully withstand intellectual anarchy and accidental serendipity?

## Too strong a box?

> The architects are aiming to identify for each 'zone' within the exhibition areas, the character of the space, the type of material it will contain, and the structural and servicing requirements.
>
> *Memo from Project Director to Curators (11.9.1991)*

The expectation of a fine building that should itself become a national icon worried curators. They were concerned that it might dominate their preponderantly small objects. Describing museums as 'our new cathedrals' at the pre-competition seminar, Marina Vaizey, *Sunday Times* art critic, had argued that the jewels mattered more than the jewel-box.[19] Dowson had concurred. Whereas a museum was 'often the architect's favourite brief, it should not be crushing, and the building should not rob objects of personality'.[20] The architects had always intended to ennoble the larger, freestanding icons. So much had been very clear from the competition drawings. It might prove a different matter for the smaller, case-bound objects whose destiny was to be slotted into walls so that the circulation spaces remained free of cases.

Moreover, objects have many different potential stories and the one selected for ennobling by the architect might not coincide with the one selected by the curator or desired by the educationalist. Would a powerful object of great aesthetic or historic quality be best highlighted as an isolated icon to receive appropriate homage, or displayed in context alongside its fellows? Therein lay the rub. In traditional museums, curators had control, and design was a service provided to curatorial requirement. Life under the Property Services Agency and its attitude to artefacts and displays, however, could be fraught, and some curators were already on the defensive in the development of the new building.[21] Philip Dowson had suggested that 'the careful construction of display ideas wedded to a design predicated upon the power of the objects themselves should produce a correct synthesis. Visitors should be confronted with great works, in circumstances that are both formal and informal .... All parts should relate to each other, and authority and authenticity should run right through it. Culture reflects the nation's attitude, and Edinburgh seems to have that confidence';[22] but it was clearly difficult for curators to come to terms with a building that expected to contribute so much to their interpretation.

The first composite exhibition brief suggested that displays should 'stimulate the visitor to explore Scotland's culture, to enjoy and appreciate what has

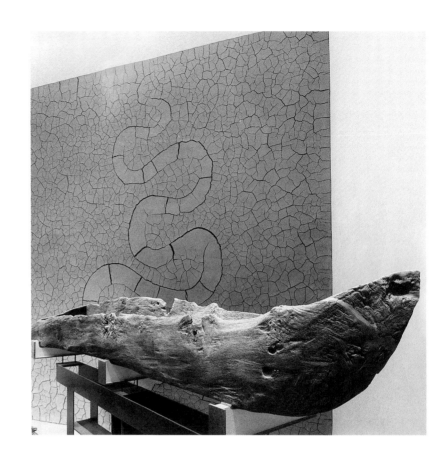

A log boat displayed in *Early People* against the clay sculpture 'River' by Andy Goldsworthy.

contributed to the making of Scotland .... We want to create a variety of experience for the visitor, in terms of message, means of display and interpretation, and pace .... We want our visitors to feel at home in the museum, but we also want to stimulate and surprise them .... The visitor could take a chronological path through [the three sections], tracing sequence and consequence, or sample according to interest and inclination .... Striking variations in scale will be as significant a feature as variations in material. Diversity, richness, and contrast will be the keynotes'.[23] Robert Anderson hoped that 'striking and intriguing' galleries would bring out the full significance of the objects on display, and relate them to their place in history or pre-history. The collection, being superb, had no need of 'acres of plastic, or designs that shout, or serried ranks of videos, or computers by the score. We don't want labels restricted to thirty one-syllable words.' He wanted sensitive, low-key, high-quality interior design, with changes of pace and variety of experience.[24]

When first invited to dream in 1986, curators' imaginations had soared. Take geology. 'The story of our exhibition is the story of the making of the rocks that comprise the landscape. We use landscape as a means of access to that story, because that is the way most people are attracted to rocks, and the minerals and fossils that comprise them, in a route with which they are familiar .... The decision was taken a long while ago that the exhibition in the Museum of Scotland would 'give the results'. It would not present the means by which those results were deduced, since that would be to expand the story too far in the space that had been allotted to geology. 'Other topics, such as Hugh Miller, have both specimens and significance to justify that larger treatment. It still seems better to fit in these individuals, and their contributions, at the place in the continuum representing the rocks that their particular work helps to explain.' There followed proposals for exhibitions on geologists, geology as a leisure activity, outstanding amateurs, teaching materials – even how geology had been used to instruct divinity students in the Free Church.[25]

### Space wars

The enormous – almost unreal – display ambitions implied by extending John Watson's School and building on this site and the southern extension were over. The first tentative exhibition draft had been to a notional 8500 m² of display space, which curators' aspirations far exceeded. Reality was to provide less than 7000 m², framed by a structure whose column grid had had to be set at 7.5 m around the larger objects long before final visions for displays had emerged.[26] Detailed design of the building had had to begin before the museum's portrayal of Scotland had matured into precise groupings of objects in defined spaces on defined routes.

It was an extraordinarily complex project. The architects were required to have an understanding of virtually every object, and a detailed one of the 200 listed as standing uncased and iconic. Since the building design was proceeding faster than the display briefs, they anxiously sought guidance. 'Life-size reconstruction of dinosaurs. Please may we have dimensions?'[27] What were the dimensions of the pipemaker's workshop, the Cornish boiler, or the Boulton & Watt steam engine? How big were the coins and were there any special display requirements? How large was locomotive 'Edina' [*sic*]? Please specify which 'additional pieces' were more than 4.5 m high. Was the Cockcroft-Walton generator still to be included? Where was robot 'Freddie' to be located? The design had to encompass, and give equal value to, a preaching tent and a sawmill engine.

Two of the icons illustrated as totemic in the original competition drawings proved incompatible with the emerging displays: the princely drawing room from Hamilton Palace and the Woodside Mill waterwheel. The Hamilton Palace display was intended to comprise three 'impressive major exhibits'. The setting was to be the panelling from the drawing room of Hamilton Palace, designed about 1701 by James Smith (who had trained at St Luke's in Rome). Robert Anderson had gone to the Bronx stores of the Metropolitan Museum of Art, New York, to open the boxes in which it lay – as indeed it had done since its purchase by William Randolph Hearst some seventy years earlier. Within the re-erected room were to be exhibited the travelling service of Napoleon's favourite sister, Princess Pauline Borghese, bequeathed to (her lover) the tenth Duke of Hamilton in 1825; and half of the tea service of Napoleon I purchased by the same Duke in 1830. Anderson thought that the conjunction of the silver with the drawing room would show that 'we do not want the boundaries of our new national museum to be too sharply drawn .... What we are displaying is Scotland as it relates to the rest to the world'.

When the Drawing Room was first inspected, Anderson enthused to *Scotland on Sunday* that it was

The Cockcroft-Walton generator, listed in the original architect's brief. There was no space for it in the area allocated for 20th-century displays.

107

exactly the kind of artefact the new museum required. 'It is wonderful to think that we can rebuild it and unveil it in Scotland, in our new national museum in the country where it originated.'[28] As the concept developed, the museum intended to purchase a 1774 portrait of the eighth Duke of Hamilton by Prud'homme,[29] to complete an ensemble intended to demonstrate to the world the hitherto unrecognised level of sophistication that had once been achieved in Scotland. But once the room arrived in Scotland, only the superlative armorial mantelpiece proved to be of the requisite late seventeenth-century period. The remainder was almost entirely nineteenth century, dating from between 1818 and 1833 and David Hamilton's stupendous transformation of the palace into the largest and finest country house in North Britain. Its quality was not in question: but it no longer suited seventeenth-century Scotland. It had been trapped in the wrong chapter of the story, and there was no room for it in the nineteenth century. Hamilton Palace was excised from the displays, and the museum contains no other interior of comparable quality.

The waterwheel had been intended to revolve like a huge, moistly dripping wheel of fortune in the south-west corner. Testing indicated that moisture would cause enormous problems in the environmentally controlled museum, and that there could be vibration. So the wheel was unhitched.[30] Into the vacuum emerged the rotunda, focused upon post-Reformation Catholic material.

## Overview

The burden of guiding exhibition and display development was delegated to an Exhibitions Review Committee, supported by a number of historical consultants.[31] Chaired first by Professor Christopher Smout, the Historiographer Royal, and then by Dr Anna Ritchie, it provided an academic overview of the display content, perceiving its task as ensuring 'that a consensus view of the past was put across'.[32] It also had the rather rockier task of mediating between display and building design. The energy expended was prodigious: phase one reports, reviews of those reports, method statements, and revision. After one presentation, for example, 'some of the specific concerns of Professors [Chris] Smout, [Peter] Jones and [Michael] Lynch' were minuted, and the proposals duly reworked. First-stage presentations were used to identify missing or poorly-developed topics – such as music, language and literature, the arts, Gaelic history and culture – and to highlight any bias. One review uncovered 'a strong bias toward the upper, lairdly and middle classes. This is partly due to the accidents of survival of material, but also reflects the choice of themes and approach.'[33] The next step was to hunt, and sometimes find, additional material that better suited the intention of the displays.

Initially, the architects had issued floor plans onto which the curators had been asked to jot the freestanding objects they wished to display. However, since the

Doorway from a house
in Kirkcaldy built into a
link between *The
Renaissance* and

*Burghs*. Through the
door is a reconstructed
room from the same
house.

latter's ideas were still evolving, 'the process is a journey, revealing unforeseen opportunities. The contents are always changing – and a museum is largely about coping with that change'[34] – they had been unable to be definitive. Sometimes the significance of objects from the existing collections was revealed through research, sometimes new objects – like the Dupplin Cross or the Cramond lioness – were added. Curators were therefore unable to predict the totality of space required early enough to influence the building process – which presented a problem for architects seeking a finite brief for a major building contract with a fixed completion date and a royal opening.

Substantial objects were to be freestanding or built into the thick walls. The remainder was contained within five different types of display cases, designed as niches within the walls. After some case layouts had been tested, difficulties with the design concept required the preparation of 'design principles for the cased displays' based upon Benson + Forsyth's generic design principles:[35] 'simple visual relationships lead to an aesthetic which allows the true focus of attention to be determined by the designer. Quite simply, if the case structure and case interior elements align in a visually simple geometric manner, they attract no attention, hence the objects on display become the main focus of attention.'[36] Fibre-optic lighting created no problem of heat gain, but access was either from the rear, or through hinged opening panels in the ash-panelled walls. 'The intent was to smother the technology.'[37]

As Phase One exhibition reports became available in 1995-6, it became clear that curatorial aspirations were still far too great for the available space. While some treasured objects were left out because display ideas had shifted or refined, others of difficult scale or dimension had to be forfeited for lack of room. The later the piece had been selected or purchased, the more limited its display options. With virtually no

Saurian footprints
of a dicynodont,
from *Beginnings*.

space left for large unscheduled freestanding objects, the only other possibility was within one of the display cases. That not only made the object much less immediate, but also excluded everything that would not fit. Similarly, the educationalists' preference for interactive exhibits that would intrude upon gallery space foundered. The strong preference for hands-on, interactive exhibitions, with flip books and objects on shelves projecting from the walls, which had only been developed after the design concept and structural grid had been finalised,[38] proved incompatible with the design.[39] Yet whereas staff tended to believe that experiments in display and interpretation were being sacrificed to the three-dimensional purity of the architectural vision,[40] that may have been the result of communication difficulties. The reality is that the circulation space was simply too small to house more freestanding objects, or to narrow it with projecting shelves. This difficult iterative process inevitably ran out of time and Trustees warned that 'the luxury of eternal revision could not be maintained'.[41] Mark Jones had reminded them 'they had commissioned a work of architecture and not an all-purpose adaptable space'.[42]

### Beginnings

Geology and ecology form the context within which people sought to create shelter, and the materials with which to make things. Don Aldridge had enthused over the original proposals: 'Forget that Scotland has some amazing petrological igneous and metamorphic freaks, forget the odd minerals like Wanlockheadite. Concentrate on the Scottishness: the fact that Scotland flipped continents, how its fossil record is so amazing because it traces the journey of a continental plate through all the climatic zones. The great contribution of Scots to geology is a bit indulgent, but people are interested in people, and I think it would appeal.'[43] But much less space was ultimately available for geology and natural history than had been originally suggested in 1987, the constriction of space being justified on the grounds that Geology and Natural History enjoyed the luxury of other galleries in the Royal Museum, and that Dynamic Earth was under construction barely half a mile away.

The location was awkwardly affected by both columns and lifts. Of the proposed displays of geologists, Hugh Miller, amateurs, and geological indoctrination of Free Kirk ministers – most had to go, although Hugh Miller now appears elsewhere. The replica coal forest in the lightwell in the north-west corner, with trees rising full height through several floors, was replaced by an aquarium with models of extinct fish. Yet even had the space been doubled, the presentation would have been loosened and the interpretation livened up[44] rather than more objects added in. 'If there is 10% too much for the visitor, it is a waste of time.'[45]

## Early People

The competition concept for the bottom floor was an arrangement of objects resembling 'an archaeological dig'.[46] Given that it was at the base of the building and was consequentially the largest uninterrupted floor-plate, the spaces were defined by the daylight running down the lightwells, so visitors would always know where they were. Claustrophobia was avoided by having structured glimpses north, through the massive chamfered columns, into Chambers Street. Powerful works of art – as was clear in the competition drawing – were arranged as befitted their iconic status.

From the beginning, the curator intended to present the material to illustrate how our ancestors were like us and driven by similar impulses. 'I want people to know that all inhabitants of Scotland are descended from immigrants; that they were quite like us, but inhabited a different world with different solutions.'[47] It implied a thematic approach rather than a chronological one. By August 1991 the theme of glass working, in terms of its messages and associated materials, was ready. 'I would like this whole document to go to the architects .... Having seen the designs for the new building, I am even more convinced that the general

A Bronze Age war trumpet or carnyx in *Early People*. It produced an enormous and haunting sound.

A 20th-century version was used to herald the royal opening of the building.

comments in this document should not be edited out in the interests of conformity through the display brief. All of us working on this immensely taxing project are going to have different approaches to providing sufficient information and highlighting the difficulties associated with our material. I can see no benefit in trying to hide these differences from the architect.'[48] The difficulty would lie in reconciling a theme that had to be followed sequentially with a design that allowed multiple access points. If visitors did not enter the gallery through the introductory area, they would be unlikely to understand how 'our conception of time as linear and precise is inappropriate at these periods when time is better viewed as cyclical and repetitive'.[49] He preferred a sequential and cheerfully didactic structure for the displays interpreting prehistoric life along a single linear route:

> There should be a circular stone enclosure representing settlements like Skara Brae at the deepest part of the building, bringing together resources and processes to display how people lived, survived, and made things: food, agriculture, toolmaking with bones, stoneworking, textiles, woodworking, metal, and glass; transport, the movement of peoples, and the exchange of goods and ideas; power and social organisation; and rituals associated with belief and death. It would illustrate how art and design were used throughout the prehistoric and early historic periods as a principal means of signalling status and identity. The more things man was able to make, the more sophisticated did his shelter become, and the more he was able to satisfy the wish and ability to celebrate season, ritual and religion.[50]

The architects' vision was that since the building's form was itself a metaphor for the historic relationship of form to organised societies, it did not need reinforcement in such a manner.[51] They produced a model to explain how their view would neither overwhelm nor distort the exhibits; but rather establish relationships between natural history, physical objects, and the outside world, through visual connections and long views to the perimeter. Architects' and Keeper's visions finally remained irreconcilable, and the gallery was replanned along linear lines.[52]

How then should visitors be greeted? It is very rare that an individual can be identified from archaeology.[53] As encountered by archaeologists, early persons are usually in the anonymous form of skeletons. Brooding on bones, the curators wondered whether a skeleton from an earlier burial could be mounted upright as a welcoming gesture. Skeletons proved *outré*, graphics would date, and silhouettes seemed somehow insubstantial. The solution lay in sculpture, which could take advantage of the fact that ancient Scots were international jewellers. Visitors are now greeted by twelve powerful, larger than life, bronze figures, created by the sculptor Sir Eduardo Paolozzi, adorned with prehistoric jewellery in the approximate way it might have been worn. These mythical Paolozzi people hint at our ancestors guarding the threshold of the first settlements.

Opposite:
Humanoid figures representing early people wearing prehistoric jewellery created by Sir Eduardo Paolozzi to symbolise the people of pre-history.

The Dupplin Cross from Perthshire, which stands at the entrance to *The Kingdom of the Scots*.

## The Kingdom of the Scots

The ambition for the ground floor gallery[54] was to provide a firm impression of Scotland whilst an independent kingdom, highlighting its political, cultural and religious life and its many marked particularities. Its themes of monarchy and power, the Reformation, the Union of the Crowns, the Covenanters, were amongst the most resonant in Scots history. Its curators gloried in the richness and colour of their artefacts. There proved insufficient display space, however, to interpret early feudal Scotland adequately, and they worried lest the rigorous consistency of gallery design display might dilute some of the objects' intensity. New ways of exploring and presenting Scottish history appeared inhibited by the formality of the design into three bays and a procession of chambers – although there was a meeting of minds, at least, with regard to the guillotine.[55] They had also wanted to extend contextualised displays into the Hawthornden Court so as to encourage visitors to move through the deep, multi-ordered door into the gallery. Without such a beacon, there was a danger visitors might not naturally do so.[56] For the time being at least, the Dupplin Cross stands guard to provide reassurance.[57]

## Scotland Transformed and Industry and Empire

The first floor gallery, opening with the Union of Parliaments, was intended to explore the eighteenth century in terms of its political and intellectual life, and social and industrial change.[58] Fourteen hundred objects, over 100 large enough to be exhibited uncased, had to be displayed in a gallery with nine entrances and exits. A strict linear or sequential circulation was thereby impossible. There was 'a multiplicity of major and minor cross-over points between different themes and groups .... Many of the same individuals were involved in numerous façets of the political, social and religious development of the eighteenth century.'[59] The material was grouped into eight themes – 'The Union', 'The Church', 'The Jacobite Challenge', 'The Spirit of the Age', 'Living on the Land', 'Power', 'The Textile Trades' and 'Trade and Industry' – to 'emphasise the inter-connectedness of things'.[60] If Scotland, paradoxically when in the political doldrums, were to be shown as a powerhouse of big ideas and practical expression, the gallery required more than just Jacobite Risings. Little could be taken for granted: 'It is astonishing how little people know about their own country.' The largest exhibit – the Newcomen engine – had since 1958 lain dismantled and boxed in store in Dundee, its rusty machinery requiring not so much conservation as revivification.[61] The engine's components represented one of the few surviving atmospheric engines in Britain. Designed by Thomas Newcomen, it had pumped water from a depth of over 160 m at Caprington Colliery, Kilmarnock, Ayrshire. The only evidence that existed of the engine pumping house was an old photograph of one façade, and drawings in the Science Museum, London. Lanarkshire was scoured for comparable examples of an engine-house; and the result is perhaps the closest synthesis in the museum between object and design presentation.

In addition to exploring the consequences of the Enlightenment through improvement and industrialisation, the displays represented some of its illuminati. Johnny Dowie, whose tavern was the home of some of the most influential Enlightenment clubs and perhaps the location of the meeting which planned the New Town; the philosopher David Hume (by a room like his); the poet Robert Burns (by pistols); the publisher William Creech (by a targe); the painter David Allan (by a gold medal); the architect Robert Adam (by model and medals); the pathologist Alexander Monro; the improver Lady Grisell Baillie; the chemist Joseph Black; the author Walter Scott (by books); the diarist Elizabeth Grant; and the agricultural improver Smith of Deanston (by a model plough). The galleries above were themed according to industry, invention and exploration in counterpoint to the consumable fruits of such endeavours. The aspiration was to convey the idea of continuity, and how history and material culture complement each other. 'If we manage to arrest somebody even momentarily, we have done well.'[62]

## The Twentieth Century gallery

In 1991 Don Aldridge had suggested that a twentieth century gallery should include a bikini found on a Spanish beach thought to belong to a Scot; the plastic cup used by Lord Bute at the opening of the museum; an osprey egg stolen by Hans Isserstadt of Westphalia; a copy of the *Daily Record* made from a plantation of sitka; and a heraldic emblem from a Chambers Street traffic warden's uniform.[63] Resonant, but altogether too whimsical. The first gallery proposal[64] was based

18th-century contrasts: the cruck-framed weaver's cottage from Croy dominated by the Newcomen engine.
*Charles McKean*

RETORTS

115

Model of the Hong Kong and Shanghai Bank, by Norman Foster and Partners, selected for the *Twentieth Century gallery* by Sir William Purves.

upon the NMS's growing twentieth-century collection. Focused upon 'within living memory' – namely work, home, personal transport, entertainment (particularly the cinema), leisure and war – the proposal started from the premise that the visitors' own experience would affect their response. A cinema auditorium, and a Memory Bank whereby people could record their memories on computer, had been selected for installation.[65] Some of the objects would have been those identified by the Twentieth Century Working Group. The architects were enthusiastically about to cantilever an Arrol Aster car above the Newcomen engine.[66]

Unfortunately, consensus on an objective perception of recent history proved difficult. Mark Jones argued that since the history was so recent, 'every visitor would be an expert'.[67] Sheila Brock, thinking it a pity to open with an empty gallery, suggested involving the public, so Mark Jones proposed putting the visitor in the position of curator. The public would be asked to consider whether future generations could understand the reality of their lives through objects they selected, just as we hope to understand the past through such objects.[68] The NMS appealed to people to suggest objects characteristic of their lives: 'What has made the biggest impact on life in Scotland in this century? What object linked with Scotland has changed your life? Why? What would you choose to become part of the story in the new museum?' There were hundreds of responses to the campaign, including fifty from well-known Scots, who had been approached directly, and fifty from staff.[69] Three hundred and forty objects were selected and every willing donor interviewed.

Mark Jones was satisfied that what had emerged from this experiment was 'a distinct viewpoint, with a techno-biased focus of what has given the individual pleasure and experience. There is less about spiritual or community endeavour than about solitary pleasures and private experiences';[70] but then it did not claim to represent the twentieth century.

COLLECTIONS EVERY THURSDAY

## Notes

1 Museums Advisory Board Report 4.7.

2 Jenni Calder: 'Social history in the Museum of Scotland' 25.1.1991. She stated to Dr David Clarke, in memo 21.8.1991, 'I feel that both Mary Queen of Scots and "Scotland and Europe" need some kind of specific focus … although I think it would be better if Mary Queen of Scots, at least, had something separate, however small.'

3 A curious view of the background of the museum's visitors.

4 Interview with Jenni Calder.

5 Dr Alexander Fenton: 'Essential Evidence' in Jenni Calder (ed): *The Wealth of a Nation*, pp 22-4.

6 Dr David Clarke to Jenni Calder 27.8.1991.

7 Information from Dr Allen Simpson.

8 Interview with Mark Jones.

9 Dr David Clarke to 1999 Heritage Conference.

10 NMS Trustees minutes 18.10.1991, items 18 and 19.

11 'Scotland's history in the National Museum of Scotland' in T Ambrose (ed): *Presenting Scotland's Story*, pp 71-2.

12 Dr David Bryden to Jenni Calder 4.11.1991. Curators had reacted adversely to the second draft exhibition brief, which appeared to move from chronology toward a more thematic pattern. MoS Exhibition sub-committee files.

13 Dr John Shaw to Jenni Calder 12.6.1991.

14 *A New Museum*, p 42.

15 Don Aldridge to Dr Robert Anderson 12.5.1991.

16 Information from Dr Allen Simpson.

17 Dr David Clarke in *Society of Antiquaries of Scotland Newsletter* 10.1, Sept 1998, p 2.

18 Gavin Sprott to Jenni Calder 23.6.1991.

19 *A New Museum*, p 48.

20 Cultural Tensions seminar; also Dr David Clarke: MoS Exhibition brief 8.5.1991.

21 Apparently, during museum design in the early 1970s, someone within the PSA's specialist exhibitions unit had begun under the misapprehension that the dimensions of the cases took priority over the length of certain African spears.

22 Cultural Tensions seminar.

23 Museum of Scotland: Exhibition Brief, second stage, introduction.

24 Anderson: 'Meeting Public Needs' in *A New Museum*, p 45.

25 Memo Ian Rolfe to Jenni Calder 13.3.1991.

26 The grid was determined on 24.1.1992. MoS Client Committee minutes 1992-5.

27 Benson + Forsyth: Exhibition Brief, second stage draft, notes, December 1991.

28 *Scotland on Sunday* 18.8.1991.

29 Memo Godfrey Evans to Jenni Calder 26.9.1991 'Hamilton Palace Display'. Calder: MoS Early Exhibitions folder.

30 A diminutive ex-colliery wheel remains in 'Scotland Transformed'.

31 That most of them were consulted far less than they had anticipated implies the success of the Exhibitions Review Committee.

32 Discussion with Dr Anna Ritchie 11.1.2000.

33 'Making & Living', Exhibition development, Museum of Scotland, Phase 1 report, p 8.

34 Evans: op cit.

35 Extrapolated and prepared by Griff Boyle.

36 Griff Boyle: 'Design Principles for cased displays', p 2.

37 Interview with Gordon Benson.

38 With the exception of 'Beginnings', where the educational aims had always been overt, and the content structured accordingly.

39 Interview with Susan Mitchell.

40 Interview with George Dalgleish. It remained his perception that the fundamental concept of the museum design had existed prior to the competition, and the difficulties arose from a mismatch of building and contents.

41 By mid 1993 the Client Committee had been informed that 'whilst the aim of achieving resonance between the building design and the exhibitions had been very successful for some parts, it had been less so in others'. Its diplomatic chairman, Professor Peter Jones, sought to ameliorate the tensions and create mutual understanding. 'He noted the tension between the permanence of the building and relative impermanence of the exhibitions …. Trustees were committed to achieving a sympathetic fit between the building and the material it was to contain. They held to their view that the new building should be a work of architecture, not a 'black box' or a shed providing infinitely flexible display spaces' (see MoSCC Minutes 24.6.1993). The following day it surfaced at a meeting of Trustees: 'Professor Smout characterised the problems as having their root in the fact that the greatest concern of the architects was the appearance of the building, whilst the greatest concern of the curators was the display of the objects', NMS Trustees Minutes 25.6.1993, item 10.

42 Ibid, item 19.

43 Aldridge, op cit.

44 Curated by Dr Michael Taylor.

45 Interview with Dr Michael Taylor.

46 Interview with Gordon Benson.

47 Dr David Clarke.

48 Interview with Dr David Clarke.

49 Memo Dr David Clarke to Jenni Calder 27.8.1991.

50 Dr David Clarke, Exhibition Brief, MoS project, First People, p 43.

51 Interview with Gordon Benson.

52 According to Dr David Clarke's linear concept by James Simpson, assisted by architects Lee Boyd.

53 Interview with Dr David Clarke.

54 Jointly curated by Hugh Cheape and Dr David Caldwell.

55 Interview with Hugh Cheape.

56 Ibid.

57 The Cross is on short term loan from Historic Scotland.

58 The curator was George Dalgleish.

59 'Making & Living', Exhibition development, Museum of Scotland, phase 1 report, p 9.

60 Interview with George Dalgleish.

61 Interview with Dr Jim Tate.

62 Interview with George Dalgleish.

63 Aldridge, op cit.

64 Developed jointly by Jenni Calder and Dr Elizabeth Goring.

65 Interview with Mark Jones.

66 Shown on the working drawings for the gallery.

67 Mark Jones: 'Temporary Display for the 20th century gallery' 27.1.1997.

68 Interview with Mark Jones.

69 Interview with Rose Watban, Dorothy Kidd and Alison Cromarty, curators of the Gallery.

70 Interview with Mark Jones.

# Delivery

Almost exactly four months after the press conference announcing the competition winner, the NMS established a Museum of Scotland Client Committee (MoSCC) to be responsible to the Trustees for the safe and effective delivery of the project. It was chaired first by Lord Bute, then by Peter Jones. Almost eighteenth-century in conception – in that several of its members had been on a museological Grand Tour accompanied by sensible tutors, and some had been part of the competition assessment – Bute intended it to exemplify patronage in action, and be prepared to take risks that normal committees might not. 'All elements of the design should eventually come to the Client Committee'[1] – every detail of the building from the sublime to the fundamental.[2] The artistic objectives of the competition brief were delegated to an Art for Architecture sub-group formed in January 1993. Commissioning of artists was something in which Bute had been accomplished, and he wanted to be certain that adequate procedures were in place should he have to stand down.

Emphasising that the exhibition design 'must be developed within the context of the overall design concept to ensure its integrity',[3] the Committee appointed a project manager as 'co-ordinator and administrator in relation to the design team's activity',[4] followed by structural and services engineers, and quantity surveyors. Specialist acoustics and lighting design consultants were tested against the brief to limit and control light levels, and to use the lowest appropriate energy whilst maximising natural light. Final selection of lighting design proved particularly challenging.[5]

Programmes were monitored, planners chivvied, and the Royal Fine Arts Commission and the Scottish Office pursued for prompt approvals;[6] but attention was focused upon the marriage of the building design and the curators' ambitions for display. Planners, generally supportive throughout, required reassurance that the Chambers Street façade, as seen from the street, would not look 'just like a blank wall'.[7] The Commission, periscope still raised, inquired signally into the silhouette and the junction between the new and old buildings; but – unwontedly benign compared to their interventions twenty years earlier – relaxed reassured. Such an ease of passage was almost certainly one of the principal harvests of the architectural competition and its technical assessment; aided by countless lectures and talks by Benson + Forsyth prior to submission for planning permission.

**" The best buildings are produced by good clients. "**

Lord Bute, to the first meeting of the Museum of Scotland Client Committee, 11 December 1991.

Opposite:
Work on the Carnegie stair.
*Niall Hendrie*

## Design development

Things were much changed from 1986. The single museum organisation had existed for virtually seven years, and it was no longer so important for the new building to underscore the unity of the National Museums of Scotland. So, at his first formal Trustees' meeting as Director, Mark Jones advocated adding an entrance to the Museum of Scotland through the drum tower, in addition to the existing entrance to the Royal Museum. A separate entrance to the new museum had been rejected in 1987 and 1991 initially on grounds of museological unity, but latterly because the experience of the winning design would be diminished if you did not enter the narrowing Hawthornden Court from the expansive Royal Museum Hall.[8] But no satisfactory way had been found to provide adequate disabled access. More importantly, 'the public would have an expectation of access at that point'.[9] Indeed it would. Much of the criticism of the competition-winning design had been on the grounds that the new museum was merely an appendage to the old one: and the growing perception of the new building as representing Scottish culture would be at odds with a building lacking its own entrance.

As it happened, an entrance through the tower had been implicit in the competition drawings. For the ground floor of the drum tower had been proposed as a shop separated from the rest of the building, oddly serviced from the rear, and the gallery behind – now the entrance hall – had been labelled 'unallocated' and left object-free in comparison to the others. It was possibly the least convincing aspect of the design. So the change required little alteration to the new museum's circulation: removal of a shop in the wrong place, and replacement of an unspecific gallery by an entrance hall. But once the tower became the entrance, it swelled in importance, adding a storey to its stature to contain a function room with stairs, lifts, cloakroom and kitchen. The roof terrace had to rise accordingly.

The adoption of a separate entrance to the Museum of Scotland was the last step in the process of ridding the new building of inconvenient non-Scottish burdens (such as the galleries for Chinese lacquer and ethnographic collections, and the Library). It was now dedicated to the single monocultural purpose stated by the Williams Committee back in 1981, of 'representing the cultural heritage of Scotland'. Even more significant was the change in circulation and the abandonment of the study galleries. Robert Anderson had defined study galleries as 'small areas providing high density displays' and 'small galleries for the contemplation of a single object',[10] but they proved to be something of a straitjacket, and militated against the narrative. In mid 1992 all study galleries were amalgamated with the main displays,[11] with the exception of 'Scottish Pottery' and 'The Silver Treasury'. A virtually spiral circulation route emerged: the two southern galleries in the tower were stepped back, new stairs were added, and it became possible to travel through

the displays in a continuous gyre over four floors, without having to double back or repeat. The spatial consequence is to make 'Scotland Transformed' a much more complex and intriguing experience.

The turnpike stair rising through the principal galleries, eventually up to the roof, was removed to the north perimeter to perform the double function of both primary circulation and escape stair – turning a 'ritualistic secondary stair into a celebration of necessity'.[12] Much grander than escape stairs and, lacking a lobby, much more immediate,[13] it is encased in the 'cathedral-class' concrete walls, cast *in situ*. Since each pre-cast tread was open, and originally detached from the wall, light could flood up and down in contrast to the enclosed ancient Scots turnpike stairs. Service access being down Bristo Port,[14] the need for a large service lift at that point created the opportunity for the large passenger lift that is now the principal access to the roof. A second large glass lift was added to the orientation cube at the entrance to the Hawthornden Court.[15]

Within the limits of a highly serviced building with sophisticated requirements for object preservation, visitor access and safety, the project was inevitably

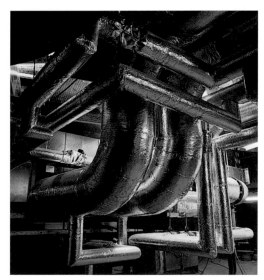

required to demonstrate green credentials. Mark Jones informed the Trustees that 'present thinking tended to question the benefits of air conditioning and close environmental control in museums. The philosophy of the new building was to maximise the extent to which the building design itself contributed to environmental buffering.'[16] Fully air-conditioned buildings were considered unsatisfactory, anti-ecological and very expensive to run. The decision – deliberately risky at the time, although now received wisdom – was to discard the museum norms [17] and opt for minimum intervention.[18] Moreover the architects wanted an engineering solution 'which produced an elegant structure and left the services invisible'.[19] Conditions within the sealed, humidity-buffered display cases would remain stable. Upper limits to heat and relative humidity were set, and the design of the thick concrete tower and curtain wall with its high thermal mass[20] was intended to assist a slow rate of change. Three air changes per hour draw fresh air from the top, filter, then cool it, before distributing it through ducts rising inside the thick walls.[21]

## Artworks

The architects expected to take a principal part in developing the art for architecture proposals,[22] identified a number of 'pivotal points on the entry route', and provided a list of other possible locations.[23] The Trustees tended toward commissioning a few special works in preference to functional items that would be required in any case. Benson + Forsyth felt strongly about the relationship of artwork to the museum. They considered that the function of art was to produce the unpredictable, and aspired to a seamless integration of art and architecture within a single aesthetic: something of the kind exemplified in the *fin de siècle* Arts and Crafts (or in the buildings of the Bauhaus, Frank Lloyd Wright or Adolph Loos), 'where architect and artists shared the same philosophy'. They did not conceive of their design as an assembly of packages, one of which might be artworks. The choice, in their view, was either artworks applied as decoration or an integration between artwork and architecture.[24] The space for the tapestry in the entrance hall, for example, was designed to rise through several volumes and be visible from a number of different viewpoints; so their brief for it was for something that could address simultaneous space rather than something that merely decorated a wall.

Gail Boardman was appointed commissions manager for the Art for Architecture Group – 'a bridge across which the ideas of the selected artists and the concepts of the architects can be harmonised'[25] – and visited the Boarbank Oratory in order to understand the architects' thinking. The next Grand Tour of architects, curators and trustees, dispatched to the Sainsbury Centre at the University of East Anglia, Norwich, the Imperial War Museum and the National Museum of Wales, was also charged to study the integration of artworks. Gradually the architects' involvement lessened, and they worried that the locations for artworks were not all as they had suggested. They were unenthusiastic about sculpture on the roof and at artists being selected on criteria other than responding to the location within the building.[26] They doubted that the artists would give comparable time to decoding their site as they themselves had given to decoding the building's site within Edinburgh. Only if they had would the piece be integral with the building and its meaning.

A few significant items were commissioned. Kate Whiteford was selected for the tapestry in the entrance hall, woven by Dovecote Studios, Andy Goldsworthy for work on the roof and in the basement, Barbara Rae for a carpet in the Bute Room, and Frances Pelly for the carved threshold stone at the point where visitors move from one museum to the other. The photographer Niall Hendrie was retained to record building activity. Crear McCartney designed stained glass for the Bute Room, contributed by the Society of Antiquaries of Scotland, and Andrew Crummy painted the construction site hoarding – followed by posters with poems by contemporary Scots poets illustrated by Edinburgh College of Art students. Sir Eduardo Paolozzi was commissioned for pieces to assist interpretation in 'Early People'. He provided the designs of his monumental manservants as a gift to the museum.[27]

## Procrustean problems

Construction is usually governed by cost, quality and time. The Trustees' starting point was to produce the new museum to the government target of £30 million excluding fitting out. They first discovered that the external stonework – desired by everybody – had been omitted from the Investment Appraisal upon which the budget had been based.[28] Then the project was hit by increases in value added tax. Eight separate times the Trustees had to agree to significant cost savings.

The NMS was not prepared to compromise the core of the competition design. Initially Bute had instructed that any reductions in the budget should, where possible, 'involve the omission of items that could be reinstated later, and would not compromise the essentials of the design'.[29] That line could not be held. Finishes were cut, staff facilities were cut, consultants' fees were cut, and various cherished ambitions – like the prehistoric coal forest – perished. The Committee's continuing insistence that nothing should be excised that would damage the design's integrity was a close-run thing. All of Bute's (and later Peter Jones') charm was exerted to maintain the *esprit de corps* including – remarkably – an apology to the design team for the unfortunate necessity of the fee cut.[30] However, when warned that a further cut in the exhibition budget would shorten the life expectancy of the displays, the Committee was steadfast: it was not prepared to relinquish 'exhibition installation

Deep foundations, begun in April 1993, helped persuade the government that the project was too far forward to be cancelled.

of a quality consonant with the aspirations of the Trustees'.[31] Luckily, the Patrons' appeal and the bid to the Lottery came to the rescue. Time, as Sir Alistair Grant informed the Trustees, was the only parameter offering flexibility,[32] and even that was constrained by a royal opening on St Andrew's Day 1998.

Given the rigour applied to design development, and the pruning of all that was superfluous or self indulgent, it seems improbable that what now had to be trimmed was needless extravagance. Rather, the true cost of the Museum of Scotland would have been 20% or more higher than the government's allotted budget: unexceptional in proportion to the total cost or to the project's importance to the country. The total cost would still have been paltry in international terms. It is doubtful whether such cost cutting was worth the effort and the potential damage to the design. Time will judge the museum on its quality. Few of those who admire the glories of the New Town of Edinburgh or the great docks at Leith recall that the city went bankrupt to pay for them.

## Start

Archaeological excavations on the site had taken place some time previously, revealing a large pit or container, presumably once used by the Renaissance brewers, and the fact that Candlemaker Row had extended eastwards to impinge on the site.

The NMS decided, given the time required to complete the appeal and all permissions, to divide the construction into four contracts. They began serially: the excavation of the basement levels; the installation of foundations begun in April 1993; works on Hall 22 to provide new offices, support accommodation, and alterations to the existing building, begun in February 1994; and the main contract. It was astute to start promptly. Government's perpetual temptation to postpone or cancel projects like this naturally increased once the severity of the recession became

124

apparent. But the early works and excavations had further heightened public anticipation, and if the project were cancelled the government would have been vulnerable to accusations of wasting substantial expenditure. It was also common sense to investigate the unknowns of the site below ground prior to letting the main contract, for it would lessen the risks of delays if something unexpected turned up during construction. Parallel working would allow construction to begin before the completion of the design.

The Trustees were particularly exercised lest the roof garden would make the museum vulnerable to damp or leaks. A suggestion that it should be roofed[33] proved even more complicated. It would not only cause significant problems of circulation and fire escape, but would also bring the building once again into the sights of the RFACS telescope. When the architects produced large-scale drawings and a model showing how the planters would be physically dissociated from the roof,[34] the plans were scrutinised minutely for unnecessary vulnerabilities. The Client Committee, dispatched to inspect Standard Life's roof garden at Tanfield, Edinburgh, reported that its impressive planting was inexpensive to maintain, and that no problems had been experienced with waterproofing.[35] The Building Research Establishment[36] reported that the flat roof system for the other roofs had a good track record, and the specialist contractor agreed to guarantee the construction of the roof.[37] So the Trustees felt brave enough to accept the roof garden as 'a vital element in the overall visitor experience'.[38] They instructed detailed design[39] and approved roof details by the end of 1993.

The NMS invited external consultants[40] to undertake a pre-tender evaluation of the technical information, the design details and the appropriateness of the contract strategy given the complications of the project.[41] Their report was based on the assumption that 'most displays would remain unchanged for long periods'.[42] It commended the strategy of putting the plant in the basement and distributing the environmental services vertically, but was scunnered by the use of stone as a rain screen. It questioned the credibility of specifying the stonework to the precision of + or −1 mm as required of the contractor. The variety of roofs and number of downpipes meant that repetition of details was rare, so the contract would require many specials at the many junctions, angles and corners of the roof. 'The building is complicated, the programme for construction complicated, and the contract documentation complicated.'[43] Given 'the inherent complexity of design', the report concluded that the building would be 'very onerous to detail and to build'. The museum would require the added security of a management contract rather than the traditional one proposed by the architects.[44]

The project managers, Turner and Townsend Project Management (TTPM), were asked to comment on the independent project evaluation and the architects to make a formal response – focusing particularly on comments about the roof and

*Niall Hendrie*

Clashach quarry, near
Hopeman, Moray.
*Niall Hendrie*

the stone. TTPM's response was bullish. The stone system had performed reliably since its introduction in the 1960s, and had withstood the extremes of the Canadian climate. The material and building systems were of sufficient standard and reliability to perform satisfactorily in the long term. The roof design detailing had been considered very thoroughly and the specification was acknowledged to be the best attainable.[45] The architects' response was brisk. The roof system was proven, as had been demonstrated elsewhere, and there were far more engineers' movement joints than had been necessary at Branch Hill. They wished to proceed to contract. The Committee accepted the architects' response and 'formally endorsed their commitment to the current design principles'.[46]

Although TTPM considered the choice of contract to be finely balanced between a traditional and a management contract, the latter offered greater flexibility in programming. Sir Alistair Grant's specialist team within the Argyll Group was firmly in favour of a management contract for such a novel and complex project,[47] and Dowson concurred. A management contract was decided forthwith, despite the potential initial additional cost.[48] Ian Hooper had to persuade the Scottish Office, which – once reassured by the strong advocacy of Grant and the Chairman – agreed.[49] Laing, Wimpey and Bovis were interviewed, their imaginations stirred, and Bovis appointed.

### Details and materials

Much excitement had been generated by the decision to use stone. Which stone? Tam Dalyell, MP for West Lothian, speedily in support of his constituents, urged the case for Binnie stone, from a quarry near Linlithgow.[50] Unfortunately the quarry was too worked out for the quantity and type of stone needed. Stone from all working sandstone quarries in Scotland was to be analysed and tested, but the use of a non-

Scottish stone (*eg* French) would require a policy decision.[51] The stone finally selected for its appearance, hardness, and weathering characteristics was Clashach, from a quarry near Hopeman, in Moray. It absorbed less moisture and resisted algae better than most. Ruddy-hued Corsehill sandstone had been selected for the slender mullions signalling the Reformed Church window, Impala granite for the plinth, and Caithness flags for the stone floors. Budget cuts then intervened, and Clashach was specified for all external stonework, and a sample was taken from every 20 m³ to ensure its consistency for this greater volume.

Stonework details, all drawn by hand at the scale of 1:20, at one time required the entire architects' office to work for a fortnight on nothing else.[52] It is not so much random as studiously varied within a rigorous control. It was mounted to a strict mathematical formula: the height of each course of stone was fixed, and the length of each panel was determined by a square, double-square or golden section, to specific ratios in each course. Thereafter, the panels could be mounted randomly. Since the architects considered that white harling would soften the precise design geometries, all façades of the curtain wall were originally intended to be stone. As part of the budget savings, the stonework on the south façade facing Bristo Street was replaced by harling.

The stone screen of the façade initially proved to be difficult and labour-intensive. Rather than solid masonry which looks as though it were holding the building up, it comprises a curtain of 75 mm thick sheets fixed to the 200 mm thick concrete wall by stainless steel brackets. Evidently outside Scottish tradition, it has open joints, slices cut through it and no copes. These emphasise its nature as a screen, a shield against the brunt of Edinburgh's wind-driven rain, which can pour through the joints and drain harmlessly behind. Traditionalists suggested it denatured the stone.[53] Trustees worried about the

Stonework detailed in the competition drawing by Benson + Forsyth.

127

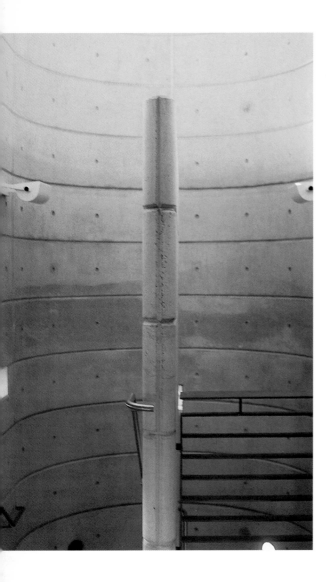

'Cathedral class' white concrete used for a turnpike stair.
*Charles McKean*

Opposite:
The white concrete underbelly of the roof structure.

algae evident on the new National Library in Causewayside and whether there was adequate experience amongst contractors and subcontractors to hang the stone precisely as drawn. They were reassured that algae growth was improbable since Clashach was a harder and less porous stone than the Library's, and the design detailing was different.[54] The issue, rather, for both Bovis and the specialist sub-contractor, Stirling Stone, was the ability of the quarry to meet the demand for the right size of stone at the right time to the right quantity.

Every small joint was given attention comparable to the major moves. White American oak was specified for doors and the long thin windows of the lift towers. White ash was used for wall linings in the galleries. The character of each part of the museum was identified by its materials, and the movement from a limestone floor to a rich Clashach floor or a beech floor signals progression and change of atmosphere. There was an almost manic attention to detail as the design team sought to extract 'pure emotive form' from the most prosaic functions. Eight years of design development had provided the opportunity for perpetual reworking. Models were even made of individual balcony seats.

The colour of the interior was to be muted, both to act as a backdrop to the colours inherent in both objects and visitors, and to allow the sun rather than paint to colour the walls.[55] So colours were generally those of the materials themselves, save where they were used to heighten perceptual awareness – in painting, for example, the exposed structural steelwork either the Forth Bridge's red oxide, or micacious grey. The sun would now fall on some 4000 m² of unpainted self-coloured plasterwork, making the plasterer's sweep more apparent. The contractor consequently used only right-handed plasterers to ensure that the application appeared consistent. Unpainted plaster not only appealed to the architects, who enjoyed using materials in their natural state, it was also cheaper.[56]

In sometimes striking juxtaposition with the russet Clashach stone, the other identifying material of the Museum of Scotland is the white 'cathedral-class' smooth concrete. Benson + Forsyth had first learnt how to specify white concrete from Tom Ellis, of the London architects Lyons, Israel and Ellis who had spent the previous thirty years experimenting with white sand and white cement.[57] They had then used it when working with Neave Brown on the housing schemes at Alexandra Road, Camden, and at Branch Hill. (The sub-contractor visited Branch Hill with the architects.) Concrete in Britain had become associated with grubby multi-storey car parks or grey, damp-stained local authority housing estates, but the constitution of the museum's concrete had nothing to do with a cheap, workaday material. It was a quality material whose distinction derived from the type of sand, the ratio of water and cement, and the care taken with the shuttering. A test project set up by the sub-contractor, O'Rourke, used shuttering of birch-faced plywood painted with four coats of lacquer. Once a sample concrete column had had to be demolished,

standards were agreed; thereafter 'normal human errors associated with a wet "on site" process were accepted as such and left as an integral part of the work'.[58] It would have been impossible to patch or infill holes imperceptibly.[59] In December 1994, Trustees learnt that the first section of white concrete had been poured and set satisfactorily.[60] Bovis' project manager told *Building*: 'It is the best finish to a concrete surface I have ever seen.'[61]

## Chambers Street

Both the competition assessors and the Trustees had been avid for the transformation of Chambers Street, into a space for events: 'We cared about this enormously. We'd have parties there.'[62] The proposed tree-lined and be-seated paved plaza extending down to West College Street, with a six-step semi-circular amphitheatre at the east end, was presented to an enthusiastic city planning officer and to Lothian and Edinburgh Enterprise in March 1992.[63] Bute considered the improvement of Chambers Street to be a vital element in making the project successful.[64] Mark Jones brought together the University, the Sheriff Courts, the Crown Office and the NMS in a group, chaired by Lord Prosser, to take the proposal forward, and the University established a Chambers Street Committee. However, instead of providing agreement and design development, the outcome was a new brief and new designer – Turnbull Jeffrey. Thereafter, in a gently evolving caucus race, schemes were suggested, disliked, amended, gnawed by the RFACS, and reworked.[65] Too many clients, too many cooks, too compromised a brief. The NMS observed despondently that improvements to Chambers Street might be out of step with the completion of the building. Just so. Barely in time for the Queen's visit, streetworks extended solely to some unremarkably widened pavements. It is curious to observe how this prodigious museum, representing an entire culture, can be designed and built faster than partial pavement widening in a non-essential educational boulevard. They arrange these things better in Europe.

# Notes

1 MoSCC 91/4, reiterated in minutes 14.1.1993: 'Lord Bute emphasised the Client Committee expected to see and approve all the details of the building .... All elements of the design should eventually come to the Client Committee.'

2 MoSCC minutes 24.1.1993. The Committee aspired to the most easily cleaned lavatories at the forefront of design.

3 Ibid 24.1.1992.

4 Emphatically *not* as design team leader. Ibid 11.12.1991.

5 The selection of lighting designers proved a recurring problem in the Client Committee minutes.

6 Concern expressed at Scottish Office delays in the appointment of consultants. MoSCC minutes 19.8.1992, and at other approvals 24.9.1992.

7 Ibid 17.3.1992.

8 The view of Sir Philip Dowson.

9 NMS Trustees minutes 31.1.1992, item 39.

10 Museum of Scotland Exhibition sub-committee minutes 28.11.1990 (4d).

11 'Conceptual brief – The Museum of Scotland project' (May 1992): Dr David Clarke stated that Dr Robert Anderson's original intention for study galleries 'had been altered by the competition brief to which the architect had responded. They had become detached' (p 10). Mark Jones was sympathetic to the concept of a fluid sequence of galleries and the integration of collections, and supported Dr David Clarke as Head of Exhibitions in making the change.

12 Interview with Gordon Benson.

13 A magnetic catch holds the door open, closing in an emergency.

14 Since the Museum of Scotland occupies the site of the Royal Museum's former loading bay.

15 After strong advocacy by Lord Perth.

16 NMS Trustees minutes 18.12.1992.

17 18° Centigrade and 50% relative humidity with tiny tolerances.

18 Information from Ian Hooper.

19 Interview with Gordon Benson.

20 MoSCC minutes 24.5.1993.

21 Ibid.

22 MoSCC 93/15: Client Committee report, October 1993.

23 MoSCC minutes 20.10.1992.

24 Interview with Gordon Benson.

25 MoSCC minutes 19.8.1992.

26 'The architects were generally sceptical about the scope for developing an integrated approach with an artist or sculptor to undertake a major work.' Ibid 19.10.1993.

27 One of the figures was gifted by the Society of Antiquaries of Scotland.

28 MoSCC minutes 4.6.1992.

29 Ibid 24.9.1992.

30 Ibid 20.10.1992, item 3.3.

31 Ibid 24.1.1993.

32 Ibid 31.1.1992 and 16.12.1992.

33 NMS Trustees minutes 22.1.1993. Whilst Ronnie Cramond suggested that a rooftop restaurant might protect the roof against leaks, Lalage Bown carried the day in favour of the roof garden and open space.

34 Ibid 16.12.1992. In March, Ian Hooper yet again invited the Committee to reconsider 'the inherent desirability, viability and maintenance implications of planting' (MoSCC 93/3). The Committee stuck to its guns.

35 MoSCC minutes 24.5.1993.

36 In reality SCOTLAB.

37 MoSCC minutes 27.5.1994.

38 Ibid, item 30, May 1993, p 40.

39 Ibid, 20.10.1992, item 3.3 21.4.1993.

40 Ove Arup & Partners, Comprehensive Design, Thomson Bethune: 'Independent Pre-tender Evaluation, Museum of Scotland', December 1994.

41 MoSCC minutes 24.11.1993.

42 'Independent Pre-tender Evaluation.'

43 Ibid, para 6.1, p 6.

44 Ibid, para 4, p 6.

45 NMS Trustees minutes 20.1.1995, item 4.2.

46 MoSCC minutes 27.1.1995.

47 NMS Trustees minutes 20.1.1995, item 4.

48 Interview with Ian Hooper. The belief was that, in the outturn, there would be no additional cost; but the appointment of a management contractor would increase costs up front, which would only prove their worth through savings and efficiency thereafter.

49 Interviews Ian Hooper, Robert Smith, Sir Alistair Grant. Also NMS Trustees minutes 6.10.1995

50 Conversation Charles McKean with Tam Dalyell, February 1992.

51 MoSCC minutes 19.8.1992. There is no evidence that this exhaustive testing of Scottish stones was carried out.

52 Interview with Benson + Forsyth office.

53 Interview with Ben Tindall and, separately, with James Simpson.

54 NMS Trustees minutes 2.5.1997, para 9.

55 Debbie Kuypers, RIBA Interiors, May 1999.

56 Ibid.

57 Interview with Gordon Benson.

58 Benson + Forsyth notes 13.7.1999.

59 Interview with Gordon Benson.

60 MoSCC minutes 16.12.1994.

61 James Macneil, *Building* 23.5.1997, p 46.

62 Interview with Lord Perth.

63 MoSCC minutes 17.3.1992.

64 MoSCC minutes 24.1.1992.

65 The RFACS had concluded that the Turnbull Jeffrey scheme failed both to respond to the functions of the street and to the quality of the environment. The MoSCC largely concurred and dispatched Gordon Benson to meet them to discuss improvements. MoSCC minutes 17.11.1995.

# The Museum of Scotland realised

You enter through a deeply recessed doorway in the three-storeyed drum tower, clad in iron-tinted Clashach sandstone, rather as you might into the great stair of the sixteenth-century palace of Huntly. Its form is lent power by its openings, and its solidity emphasised by its double skin. Once inside however, you are not in a great staircase but a hollow circular anteroom or porch, rather like a Galilee chapel to a cathedral. It feels much bigger than you might expect from the outside – accentuated by its recessed toplit seats within battered fat walls. It is as though it has its own scale. Being circular, the imagery is that of a very sophisticated broch, ashlar walls up to dado height, and plaster above. Unlike a broch, you cannot move upstairs from the ground level, and the gloriously curved staircase that lies within the wall between the upper floors is completely imperceptible.

You cross a bridge into the cavernous double-height entrance hall, flanked on the right by a powerfully plain wall, stone up to dado height, and the Kate Whiteford tapestry on the left, hinting at unseen floors above. The space is split by an ash and plaster balustrade between ramp and steps. Three sculptured Caithness slabs carved with whorls and spirals of names by Richard Kindersley stand to the left. As you cross the bridge (over the archaeology a storey below) into the Hawthornden Court, you face a vision of Venice. The beautifully restored arcaded western flank of the Royal Museum west pavilion acts as the east wall to the much-debated junction between the new and old buildings: a curiously expansive space framed also by the white and glass lifts and by the huge north window. The schools' direct access into the new museum shown on the competition drawing had become redundant with the new entrance, and the window provides access for large objects, swings open as a fire door, and provides an air intake for the emergency smoke extraction system.

The Hawthornden Court – more than 'a three-dimensional courtyard – a deep breather'[1] – is the focus of the entire design: the orientation space, the agora, the meeting place and the great void down onto which you get glimpses from the galleries. It is the setting for events. Taller, narrower, brighter and more echoing than the Royal Museum's great hall, it lacks the latter's lacy iron columns and the undidactic cheerfulness of its glass umbrella. It is altogether more Presbyterian. Reached by bridges to emphasise how it is 'disassociated from the surrounding buildings by its edges',[2] the Court is the fulcrum between the orthogonal geometry of the Royal Museum to the east and the medieval indiscipline lying through the

**"Contents of a self-respecting museum: a small winding corridor for conversations; offices all of the same size; secondary offices where curators can write their coffee-table books; exhibition space for cancelled shows; snooker room for attendants; huge underground display space for vehicles of senior workers; palatial dining room for a quick Royal drink once a year; left luggage room; huge vault for the bulk of the collection; offices for people to look after the huge vault; a secret door; an incinerator for unsold catalogues; a large wine cellar."**

Miles Kington, *Independent*, 22 August 1992.

**"We are not permanently beside our buildings to explain them. They have to speak for themselves."**

'Mecanoo': RIAS Convention, 1998.

Opposite:
The southern gallery of the Hawthornden Court.
*Niall Hendrie*

133

window to the west. 'The desire was for a non-rectilinear courtyard which we treated as though it had external surfaces; it is the outside inside.'[3] The floor is stone; the rising stair is clad in stone (ash-walled inside), high walls otherwise plastered. Far above, as there might be in the closes of Edinburgh, there are three viewing platforms from the galleries facing across to the curving posterior of the restaurant's servery. They exemplify Mackintosh's praise for 'the extraordinary facility of our style in decorating construction, and in converting structural and useful features into elements of beauty'.[4]

The 'close' stairs descend gently from the Hawthornden Court to what should seem a basement. Yet with light filtering down the lightwells onto a limestone floor, and flooding in from the columned screen facing Chambers Street, it is obviously much more than that. Its power is immense: at once subterranean, a chambered tomb, and a laigh hall, it catches that elusive sense of authority implied by the great monuments on display.

In this rich tomb-like womb-like space, geology, natural history and archae-ology act as the cultural foundation for what rises, growingly confident, above. Facing the stair, on a slightly elevated platform abutting the Royal Museum, 'Beginnings' explains the geological formation of Scotland. Emphasising the identifying feature of Scotland's culture – the stone, the geology, the geography, the wildlife and the weather – it was designed to depict Scotland's pristine environ-ment just before the first farmers arrived 650 million years ago. Starting with an introduction to the history of Scottish land, showing how Scotland has moved across the world, the display opens with huge rocks to signal the immensity of geological time. The best objects – including some new objects, like the 'not very attractive'[5] Lizzie from Bathgate, the fossil of the first amphibian – are used to tell the story. Unable to present a saurian panorama, the curators have chosen sandstone with a footprint. Because its space is residual and largely architecturally neutral, 'Beginnings' has a freedom less evident in the other galleries. Trails can

Diorama in *History of the Wildlife*, showing the Arctic tundra of the last ice age and the forest that replaced it.

View west through *Early People* past the Cramond lioness and up to the Hawthornden Court.

be followed, and objects stroked. The history of Scottish wildlife beyond, its survivals and extinctions, features a diorama depicting the Scottish landscape, flora and fauna just before humans emerged to transform them.[6]

'Early People' occupies the remainder of the 'laigh hall', and as you move downstairs to them, you are greeted by ranks of powerful Paolozzi manservants. The majestic colonnade of monumental tapering oval columns to the right frames views outside, allowing glimmerings of summer evening sun, offset by relics illuminating the 'belief systems of invaders' – Roman stones, early British, Christian and Pictish stones. Beyond the Cramond lioness munching her early person, and a burial sunk into the floor, you descend even further into the ground, into the circular sepulchral subterranean chamber at the foot of the drum tower. Behind it lies a small concrete wedge-shaped lecture theatre: a reinterpretation in concrete in a similarly subterranean location of Charles Rennie Mackintosh's lecture room below the Glasgow School of Art. But it lies beneath neither tower nor museum, but beneath the gap between the two, hence the curving wall on one side (the tower) and splayed wall on the other (the museum).

An entrance on the left through the thick wall, symbolising the base of the tower of galleries above, leads into the thematically organised route through the archaeological collections. The first encounter, almost as an ante-chamber, is with a slate broch created by the sculptor Andy Goldsworthy from 66,000 roofing slates. Tactile walls curve like an enormous grey cat. Along the bays of the south wall, he also created the bay-sized clay panels etched with designs of circles or rivers as backdrop for exhibits of ironwork, glassworking, shelter, and transport. They re-affirm 'that there are still among us individuals with the same awareness, knowledge, and appreciation of the natural environment that was second-nature to prehistoric peoples'.[7] The 'wider horizons' section, beyond the core tower to the east, offers gaunt views to the sky five levels above.

Turning back toward the entrance, the austere space, light to one side, dark to the other, and populated by symbol stones as mythical as Paolozzi's people, creates a tangible sensation of almost-present ancestors.

Upstairs lies the world of better-recorded history. The ceremonial entrance into 'The Kingdom of the Scots' had been thickened and ennobled since the competition and, for the time being, is heralded in mythic majesty by the Dupplin Cross. The diminutive timber St Andrew and the tiny Brec Bennoch of St Columba – survivor of Bannockburn – beckon from within. The north aisle, nearest to the Hawthornden Court, like two fat-walled interconnecting state apartments, contains 'Monarchy and Power' – the Stewart Dynasty and its tormentors, warfare, firearms and 'institutionalised cruelty'. The far aisle, addressing life and trade in the burghs, displays domestic items with domestic lighting in the cosy scale provided by the mezzanine, which is reached by the wheel stair carved into the wall. Doors, door

The Monymusk reliquary, 'the tiny Brec Bennoch of St Columba', one of the smallest and most resonant objects displayed in the museum.

Displays in 'A Generous Land' contained within a slate broch by Andy Goldsworthy.

lintels and heraldic panels are inserted into both structure and route. The museum's conservation philosophy being one of reversibility, it would not emulate the Burrell's cheerful incorporation of large architectural works into its fabric. The challenge for conservators was to make these doors and lintels seem as though they were built into the fabric, whereas they in fact sit in invisible steel cages within the fat walls.[8] They could be removed, albeit laboriously, should there be a major redesign of the gallery.[9] The vast bulk of exhibits are contained within five different types of display cases, designed as sunken niches within panelled or plastered walls. The white ash panelling is invariably aligned with the cases, door lintels, or other geometric intrusions.

Small-scale items of sophisticated urban use – food, corn, wine, pipes and pistols – act in counterpoint to the large freestanding panels from Mary of Guise's Edinburgh house. While there was no intention to recreate a room from bits, the way the objects are disposed nonetheless creates powerful echoes of how once they might have been used. The central bay conveys the impression of a 'great hall' at the centre, bounded to the east by 'Na Gaidheil' ('The Gael', including the 'Lordship of the Isles'), and to the west by 'New Horizons' – the seventeenth century. Lined with doors, panels, chests, cabinets and selected icons, its scale rather overwhelms the ceiling from Queen Mary's Room in Rossend Castle. Lacking its spatial frame, it goes largely unremarked.

To leave town life and trade, you can cross a bridge over the light well onto the gallery of 'The Medieval Church' to gaze at another sepulchre below. The creation of the kirk, its curving painted ceiling slotted beneath an invisible car and bicycle park, gave the architects deep pleasure. Steps down to the softly-lit crypt 'which resembles the original environment, with a spiritual dimension'[10], parallel those down to the semi-subterranean Blackadder Aisle of Glasgow Cathedral or the semi-subterranean choir chapel at Rosslyn. Higher level lighting is focused on objects as though they were candle-lit. A window peeping through into 'Early People' offers a glimpse of an even deeper past. The route then moves up and round the perimeter into the brightly-lit rotunda – carved bosses hanging from the ceiling – where the scale and light explode as a prelude to entering 'The Reformed Church'. At a winter's noontime, a cross of sunshine from its cruciform south-facing window illuminates the floor. You may choose to cross another bridge, back into 'New Horizons', with a vista back to the gallery entrance and to St Andrew, or to continue round the corner to 'The Reformed Church', where translucent light filtering between the painstakingly designed window mullions increases in intensity. The standard window system lies buried beneath high craftwork, and even the window transoms are lined with ash. From the National Covenant on its wall, you may gaze westwards to the sturdy gable of Greyfriars Kirk where it was signed.

The architectural journey governs our perceptions. The majestic Hawthornden

Steps, rising from the Hawthornden Court with its landings and platforms, its balconies, viewing points and seats, and its carefully contrived vistas, views and glimpses, makes you sense that you are nearing the top of the building. You begin to expect an attic. You cannot see what lies behind the wall on the right. A shock waits as you turn into 'Scotland Transformed'. You have arrived in no attic, but at the foot of a huge machine, appearing to soar up through countless other storeys to other rooflights or clerestoreys, like something from the film 'Metropolis'. It is the Newcomen engine in its stone overcoat, with beams of a scale to require entire trees. Just in front is the diminutive extract of a heather roofed, soot-smelling, cruck-framed Dunbartonshire cottage from Croy. Jacobitism lies unannounced to the left. That so little of its industrial collection could be displayed in the museum is rendered largely irrelevant by this stupendous architectural device. Nobody arriving up that great staircase will leave the museum without having the power of industrial Scotland firmly impressed upon their subconscious. The knowledge they will take away will provide the context within which they might enjoy Lead Mining, Maritime or Mining Museums at Wanlockhead, Irvine or Prestongrange. More-over, it is very much a display of our time: an exhibition 100 years ago would have made commensurately more of Jacobites and less of machinery.

Relocation of the original turnpike stair in the galleries to the north enables you to enter the gallery from the rear, directly into 'The Spirit of the Age', through the drawing room from Riddle's Court. Although the less dramatic way of reaching the gallery, it provides the more dramatic thematic sequence; through the window of this doucely furnished early eighteenth-century room, you can glimpse both a country cottage and the footings of an industrial Leviathan, looming like Baal, or the statue of Athene in the Acropolis. The intimate space beneath the mezzanine, semi-screened from the machinery beyond, is a timber-floored gallery with domestic furniture – grandfather clock, Francis Brodie furniture, and a sedan chair as counterpoint to cased displays (or niches); and the re-erected room from Riddle's Court, Edinburgh. David Hume had lived there before moving to St David's Street in the New Town (anecdotally named after him by the postman). What is on display is a coherent arrangement of objects that would have been used by the Enlight-enment illuminati, seen by, worn by or read by them, conveying a sense of their discernment.

The gallery conveys the might of industrial power – hand-power, water-power, and steam-power. The theme 'the Jacobite Challenge' at the east end of the gallery would not, of itself, have given an adequately broad perspective of eighteenth-century Scotland, for so much else was happening. So the exhibition of Jacobite material, including the banners of the Appin Stewarts and of Barrell's Regiment which faced each other at Culloden, Bonnie Prince Charlie relics, and material from the various rebellions, inhabit the apse of an enormous, almost Victorian,

The silver gilt canteen which belonged to Bonnie Prince Charlie, part of the display on the Jacobite risings. It has a delicacy rather overwhelmed by the industrial machinery on the same floor.

The same model of the Bell Rock lighthouse built by Robert Stevenson illustrated on page 24. This part of *The Workshop of the World* has views through to *Made in Scotland* in a parallel gallery.

turbine hall, with ranks of cases of craftsmanship, colliery models and foundry ladles. One eighteenth-century tartan army at one end; and the hint of a different tartan army emerging from the link between the textile trade and the ceremonial visit of King George IV to Scotland in 1822 at the other. Spatially, it implies that romantic Jacobitism was a sideshow to the growth of the cannily exploitative industrial Scot. The contrast between the cruck house – a typical rural workplace as much as a home – and the Newcomen engine symbolises the enormous changes that took place in the Scottish rural economy. Small items for display cases jostle things against walls, icons and the museum's larger pieces, a beetling machine, the Corliss valve steam engine and handlooms.

Across the close or lightwell to the south lies 'The Church', a double-height rooflit, sidelit space, which displays communion plate, a pulpit, a Moderator's gown, an oak screen and a stool of repentance. It explores the 1843 Disruption and some of its consequences. The south turnpike stair can carry you up to the gallery above, with its emphasis upon death and its rituals – headstones, tombstones, funeral processions, funeral hatchments, and the Bolton hearse. Moving beyond 'The Church' round to the west, past the gothic stained glass window by Douglas Strachan which blocks the southern view down into the lightwell, you enter 'The Textile Trades'. Half-way along, a seating niche projects from the plane of the building over the pavement below, a tiny place of privacy (reminiscent of the one in the upper corridor of Mackintosh's Hill House) giving long glimpses north and south. As you cross the lightwell back east, a vertiginous view opens up of the wall of the Hawthornden Court.

'The Workshop of the World' lines the south side of the 'turbine hall' at a level half-way up the Newcomen engine. Here are more industrial icons: the whisky still, the *Ellesmere* locomotive, bridges, ship models, and an eclectic collection of Scots-made products from lathes to lavatory pans. A wide flight of timber stairs leads up to displays of some of the rewards and consequences of such industry. The stairs, debouching just where the apsidal stair and the lift exit meet, end in the Scottish diaspora: where Scots went, and the impression they made on America, Australia and New Zealand. The focus of the floor, however – the way Victorians and Edwardians lived, consumer goods, urbanisation, immigration, tea-rooms, fashion, and arts and crafts – extends round the perimeter, save for two collections projecting into the hall below – a circular drum (resonant of a kiln) containing pottery, and a cube (resonant of a treasury) containing silver. Casual visual snapshots into the 'turbine hall' to the south contrast with the breathing spaces perforated through the northern wall – the high-level balconies overlooking the Hawthornden Court. The ruddy-hued engineering gantry on the south side – deliberately resembling a section of the Forth Bridge[11] – provides the immensely rich experience of looking down through three separate galleries and many different themes, very rarely available in a museum. It displays innovators and inventors. The constant intertwining of small scale to large scale, domestic to industrial, is never used to better effect.

Benson + Forsyth were only commissioned to produce a shell for the Twentieth Century gallery, since it was planned to be used for changing exhibitions. A 'space for the future' differentiated from the carefully crafted nature of the unchanging galleries, it is generally white with beech floors and a limestone surround. The interior wall to the west is on a shallow curve, creating tension, and slit windows on the other side give focused glimpses of the Castle, Heriot's Hospital and the Infirmary. In form, the gallery resembles those of the Royal Museum, being a perimeter gallery running round the roof level, top-lit by circular rooflights. The display, designed by Graven Images and by Association of Ideas, is more like a temporary exhibition than a permanent museum

Twentieth-century objects chosen by members of the public. In the foreground two Peugeot mountain bikes dated 1995 and 1998.

141

Bridge across the Hawthornden Court linking *Scotland Transformed* to the tower.
Charles McKean

A floodlit view of Edinburgh Castle from the Board Room.

display. In place of tableaux prepared by curators to explain context, the objects are generally treated as isolated pieces within broad themes. It has a linear structure, in which the objects are grouped thematically – home, play, leisure, sport, war, politics, health, technology, education and national identity. 'What you will see in the 20th-century galleries is what you get if you ask people what is important to them by way of real objects: national identity, space, travel and computers.'[12] The chosen object might be a machine – like the washing machine, which has helped everybody (a major twentieth-century change being the easing of domestic chores) – alternative forms of energy, robotics, or a personal choice significant to a particular family. It was not all celebration. Some chose the bomb or an aerosol can, and two teachers selected a tawse.

Context is replaced by text written by the nominator of the object: 'School-children are no longer ink-stained, thanks to Lazlo Biro. He was a Hungarian, living in Argentina, who invented the first working ballpoint pen. It became popular in the United Kingdom in the 1930s, superseding the scratchy metal nib stuck onto a wooden holder that one dipped into a well filled with ink, drowned insects and the like.'[13] National identity is represented by ship and airline tickets, the Scotland Bill, a ballot box, voices, tartan, a flag and Irn-Bru which 'cures the hangover from Scotland's other drink'.[14]

The tower is reached by the bridge across the Hawthornden Court, the Discovery Centre lying to the right. The first floor of the tower is entirely occupied by the Bute Room, a powerful drum with fat, white curving walls, and a vivid carpet by Barbara Rae, inspired by the Lammermuirs and woven by Dovecote Studios, sunk into the floor. The carpet best exemplifies the architects' aspirations for the integration of art and architecture – namely that in the commissioning and placing of such artworks, the joints would be invisible.[15] Crear McCartney's tall and thin stained glass window faces west.

Upon entering the Bute Room, the purpose of the great gash north-west becomes apparent. The far wall of the room appears to be closed by the dull brown and red sandstone walls of George IV Bridge's shops and offices. There is no initial view of the Castle, since underlying the architectural approach was a belief in the value of the 'accidentally disclosed vista'. To reveal everything at once would have devalued the experience. The view would have been too obvious – 'instantly consumable; monosyllabic'.[16] As you approach the window to overlook George IV Bridge, the view west begins to emerge and, above the brown and red stone, the profile of Edinburgh Castle.

Within the thickness of the west wall, broch stairs rise to the Board Room, designed as 'the conclusion to the building'.[17] Benson + Forsyth, unusually, spelt out their design intentions in detail:

> The Board Room is unquestionably one of the most important spaces in the building, and in our view is critical to the totality of the Museum, as is the Director's Office in Mackintosh's Glasgow School of Art. The views from the room have been carefully defined to provide an extraordinary frame to the Castle and the setting sun to the west, a complete vista the length of Chambers Street and, as one descends the staircase, a controlled focus to Middle Meadow Walk and the Pentland Hills beyond. Orientation was to represent, in this one space, the entire building in microcosm …. The architecture of the room is derived therefore from the architecture of the building itself. The development of the walls, furniture and soft furnishings should belong to the family of the building …. Each element of the space contributes to a satisfactory acoustic balance – *eg* the absorption factor of the canvas cushions to the built-in sofas.

Considering the aesthetic qualities of standard acoustic ceilings to be meagre, they designed a ceiling screen of white ash slats beneath which sound-absorbing material is concealed. Recessed into the double-thickness walls, seating benches snuggle comfortably into niches.

The broch stairs continue up, now exposed to the weather, past a stunning mullioned window – almost an eyrie facing westwards over George Heriot's Hospital – to the top floor terrace, with its substantial planters. Sliced stone lancets are cut through the parapet facing east, west and north providing a distant echo of crenellations.

Edinburgh reflected in the clerestory beneath the roof garden. The circular roof lights illuminate the *Twentieth Century gallery.*

Soaring high above the Newcomen engine, a bellying white curved form, like the keel of a boat or the underside of a great white whale, heralds the roof garden above – so fundamental to the ordering of the building and so hard fought for. The roof is reached principally from the Bristo tower – the lift at the south-east corner concealed in the powerful rectangular caphouse, stone clad to the north and harled on its other three sides (as once was George Heriot's). It provides the slender vertical climax sought by the Cockburn Association originally absent from the winning design. The enormous window of the lift lobby, with its simple cruciform mullion, sucks in the prospect as though you were in an osprey's nest. 'In the sun, the view is lovely. The sun bounces off buildings giving you dynamic shadows.'[18] The straight stair, rising within thick walls at the centre, its walls sliced for that view to the Polar Star (a faint gesture to the planetarium that, generations ago, had been planned for that location) is a good route down.

The roofs of the Museum of Scotland, representing its 'fifth façade', needed to appear as 'positive objects'[19] – hence the storm prow at the apex of the Hawthornden Court jutting from the west façade; hence the roof garden with its smooth white hull. The view from the roof is undifferentiated and open, save for the wide, axially placed, horizontally proportioned white belvedere, facing east to North Berwick Law. Straight on, it frames Edinburgh University's dome; obliquely, it frames St Giles or, *per contra*, Arthur's Seat.

Opposite:
The great mullioned window of *The Reformed Church* facing out towards Greyfriars.

## Notes

1 Interview with Gordon Benson.
2 Ibid.
3 Ibid.
4 Charles Rennie Mackintosh: 'Scotch Baronial Architecture' in P Robertson (ed): *Charles Rennie Mackintosh, the Architectural Papers.*
5 Interview with Dr Michael Taylor.
6 Devised by Dr Andrew Kitchener, Curator of Mammals.
7 Clarke: *Antiquaries' Newsletter*, op cit, p 2.
8 Interview with Dr Jim Tate.
9 Ibid. The same could scarcely be said of the *Ellesmere* engine, the Newcomen engine or some of the other larger objects.
10 Interview with Gordon Benson.
11 Ibid.
12 Interview with Mark Jones.
13 Caption submitted by I A Nimmo.
14 Caption submitted by G J Moonan, and included as part of 'cultural identity': 'as a country partial to the odd libation, could this amber antidote for a hangover have been invented by anyone else? This sweet nectar must have saved more lives on a Sunday morning than the chicken pox vaccine'.
15 Interview with Gordon Benson.
16 Ibid.
17 Letter Gordon Benson to Mark Jones 15.5.1998.
18 Interview with Gordon Benson.
19 Ibid.

# Envoi

**"This building will define a nation."**

*Sir Philip Dowson*

What should a national museum look like? In 1972 it would have been a modernist, columned rectangle highlighting each floor level. In 1988 it would have been a sleek, geometric box with metal panels. Neither building would have been expressive of its contents or purpose; only of its structure. Nor was there any obvious intention to be 'Scottish'. Ten years later, the Museum of Scotland's expression had become fundamentally cultural if not national. The simple, neutral shiny pavilion implied by the Feasibility Study had been transformed into a metaphorical design, each element implying something about its location, or its function, or about Scotland. Mechanical elements were to be visible only where they contributed to the museum's narrative; otherwise suppressed or concealed within the profiled stone.

The brief's requirements for main, flexible galleries and satellite study galleries had been resolved with a plan resembling those of Gàidhealtachd strongholds, appealingly illustrated on the original competition entry by Dunstaffnage. But it was still a modern museum plan – and, in any case, Edinburgh is not even in the Gàidhealtachd. The castle-like inheritance might include a curtain wall and round corner tower, but whereas Dunstaffnage is built of rubble, the 'randomness' of the sophisticated stone sheets of the museum was achieved only with immense care. The 'tower house' of galleries is capped by a roof garden sitting on a boat's hull, with a lifthouse in place of a caphouse. Whatever the parallels with historic precedents, any resemblance can only be a matter of cultural memory. When Charles Rennie Mackintosh presented Walter Blackie with the Hill House, he stated, 'Here is the house. It is not an Italian Villa, an English Mansion House, a Swiss Chalet or a Scotch Castle. It is a Dwelling House.'[1] The Museum of Scotland is not a Gàidhealtachd stronghold, an Edinburgh close, or an Enlightenment monument. It is a late twentieth-century location for Scottish displays.

Without the determination of the Earl of Perth, and the Marquess of Bute's subtle, wily but dogged pursuit of the goal of a worthy national museum for Scotland's treasures – 'the sanctuary of national pride' that he had trumpeted quietly in 1982 – the Museum of Scotland might never have been built. To a degree it is built to their concept. Bute's final contribution was to invite Ian Lang, then Secretary of State, to dig the first sod on 30 April 1993. Typically diffident and good-humoured, he had been suffering from cancer for over two years, and had undergone painful operations. Awarded the KBE in the June Honours List, he died on 21 July that year. NMS Trustees acknowledged that 'without his personal commitment,

A visitor between lighthouse and ship model in *The Workshop of the World*.
*Niall Hendrie*

147

the Museum of Scotland would not have emerged as a reality',[2] and the manner in which he exercised that commitment was widely admired. 'John Bute civilised everything he touched, and with such grace that everybody enjoyed doing it with him.'[3] A measure of his footprint was the throngs who attended the Memorial Services held in London and in Edinburgh. Obituaries suggested that one of his most striking memorials would be the Museum of Scotland; and it had been Bute's idea that the process of achieving it should be recorded in a book.

It looks as though no government would ever have been prepared to fund the full construction ambitions of the two former museums. The judgment of the two museums' expert staff that there would be insufficient space for them both on the Chambers Street site proved entirely superfluous. The government was barely prepared to stump up for a building in Chambers Street. Failure to admit this openly caused decades of expensive effort wasted on corrosively abortive work – which, if valued correctly, would probably have cost a sum equivalent to the savings it thought it was making. More germane to ministers' views was limiting public expenditure. The elaborate charade of 1954-76 demonstrated the impossibility of two separate institutions sharing the same inadequate plot, and revealed beyond doubt that if it were to be Chambers Street and nowhere else, the two museums would have to be merged. Since there is no evidence of logic in the ministers' original decision-making, the formation of the National Museums of Scotland was the inadvertent benefit of questionable decision-making.

The character of the site – at the meeting of five streets, a memory of an ancient gate into Scotland's capital city, and the juxtaposition of organic old Scotland with rationally enlightened North Britain – governed the architectural response. All the influences emerging from its environs were synthesised into a powerful building which exemplifies 'Greek' Thomson's belief that 'the laws of architecture do not consist in a series of arbitrary contrivances. They were not invented by man, but merely discovered by him'[4]; a Scottish certainty in an uncertain world.

Three themes dominated the development of the Museum of Scotland: the compression of material into insufficient space; the requirements of a national narrative as against the display of collections; and the extent to which the building – the narrative's armour, as it were – should be part of the exhibition and influence our perception of the exhibits. The site proved so three-dimensionally challenged as to be insufficient even to satisfy the curatorial ambitions of the new merged organisation. It required the 'Museum of Scotland' concept to change – from being the sole depository to being a 'mother' site, and signpost for material elsewhere. Its national network includes the National War Museum of Scotland in Edinburgh Castle, the Museum of Flight at East Fortune, the Museum of Scottish Country Life in preparation at Wester Kittochside, East Kilbride, and the Museum of Costume at Shambellie House, Dumfriesshire. Furthermore, the NMS has shifted from the position

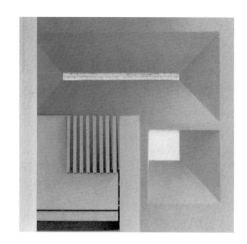

of remoteness, of which the Williams Committee accused its predecessors, to one that gladly contemplates sharing material. It has curated and supplied displays in other museums – such as the displays in the Museum of Piping in Glasgow – and, when the Museum of Scotland opened, there were 150 current loan agreements with other institutions.

The process of its creation proved perplexing even beyond difficulties of site. In 1990 Sir Philip Dowson had warned the NMS that 'the creation of a building encompasses experiences of many kinds. It is born of passion, effort and dedicated attention'[5] – a coded warning that it was unlikely to prove painless. Nor was it. It was a building whose purpose, form and content were novel, with little to draw on by way of relevant precedent. The client was a new institution, without experience in making decisions of quite of this kind before. A fluid concept like 'representing the nation's culture' might normally take decades to determine, yet construction decisions were required only four years after it was first considered. It should not have been unexpected that the formalisation of the design and structure would jar against unresolved conceptual uncertainties. A building project with all these features was likely to prove challenging, requiring courage, sympathy, excellent communications, good backing, and above all mutual understanding.

There is no such thing as a risk-free *grand projet*, whatever mechanisms timorous governments and fee-hungry management acolytes put in place. Funders of building projects understandably seek a programme for its construction, and processes put in place to achieve it. Yet these are only man-made yardsticks, and they are changeable. A building is not necessarily a failure if either is disturbed. Perspectives of time and perceptions of opportunity also change. In the creation of the Museum of Scotland, the hazards extended far beyond construction to embrace the complications of politics, interpretation, understanding and delivery. There were the assimilation pains of two different cultures, a new idea and a new organisation to be embraced. Museology was changing, and the ever-mutating concept of what was meant by 'Scotland' had to be pinned down. Nor is there any architectural Esperanto or common language to assist mutual understanding when architects have a vision and curators parallel ones. Indeed, Trustees and staff took on trust the architectural vision long before they could themselves appreciate its reality, and became aware of its implications. In the face of angst, Sir Alistair Grant pointed out how important it was to remember that 'everybody was doing what they were doing in good faith'.[6]

The move from a collection-based museum to a narrative museum proved particularly taxing, especially once the spatial consequences for exhibition of design decisions emerged. Display proposals were only fully developed by the time design and construction had advanced too far for any but marginal modifications. The Hamilton Palace Drawing Room had fallen victim to space and time. There

Donald Dewar, shortly to
become Scotland's First
Minister, and Sir Robert Smith,
Chairman of NMS Trustees,
inspecting the building.

had been space for it, but only in the wrong time: a nineteenth-century interior seeking shelter in a seventeenth-century location. However, as the building took shape, new objects replaced discarded objects and displays began to assume their final character, so was the depth, scale and clarity of the architects' concept better understood, then appreciated and finally admired.[7] You only have to contrast the museum with what the PSA previously designed for the site to understand how far Scotland has travelled since 1976.

Gordon Benson, Alan Forsyth and their team spent eight years obsessed with the design of the Museum of Scotland and its every detail. In the face of budgetary pressure, Trustees had had repeatedly to protect the core of their design as had been promised at the competition assessment: 'The Committee wished to ensure that the integrity of the building design was not compromised.'[8] Although each change, development or cut meant that more had to be made with less, the architects found it a creative process. Most of the fundamental post-competition design developments – particularly the changes to the circulation – proved to be to the building's benefit. That the museum so closely resembles the original design implies success and a rare level of commitment to patronage; and participation in the making of the Museum of Scotland was likely to be considered, retrospectively, the high point in the career of those involved.[9] The NMS Chairman concurred. 'It is not given to a lot of people to be involved at such a level on such a wonderful project.'[10] The building was opened by the Queen, in a condition of approximate completion, on St Andrew's Day 1998.

The National Museums of Scotland, conceived under sixteen years ago, has proved a sturdy, if self-willed, creature, whose adolescence was protracted by the maggoty firesale of the land to the south. The principal aspirations of the Museums Advisory Board – the creation of a single museum organisation, the creation of a Museum of Scotland, and the development of a new role for the museum in relation to the rest of Scotland – have been achieved. The NMS has shown itself to be a patron, confident in itself and in its relationship with other museums. The core of the hard-won competition-winning design for the Museum of Scotland building did indeed emerge unscathed, as the competition assessors pledged in 1991; and the quality of the new building standing sentinel at the end of Chambers Street has attracted international attention. Bute's ghost is likely to be paternally pleased.

## Notes

1  Walter Blackie: 'Memories of Charles Rennie Mackintosh' in *Scottish Arts Review*, vol II, 1968, pp 6-11.
2  MoSCC minutes 29.7.1993.
3  Interview with Sir Philip Dowson.
4  Alexander Thomson, Second Haldane Lecture, in G Stamp (ed): *The Light of Truth and Beauty*, p 125.
5  Sir Philip Dowson: 'The Architect's Role' in *A New Museum*.
6  Interview with Sir Alistair Grant.
7  Interviews with Sir Alistair Grant, Sir Robert Smith, Mark Jones.
8  MoSCC minutes 6.10.1994.
9  Interview with Mark Jones.
10  Interview with Sir Robert Smith.

# Sources

## Published books

Douglas Allan (ed): *The Royal Scottish Museum 1854-1954* (Edinburgh 1954).

Timothy Ambrose (ed): *Presenting Scotland's Story* (Edinburgh 1989).

I A Bercedo Puyuelo and I Sen: *The architecture of museums* (New York 1997).

Iain Gordon Brown: *The Hobbyhorsical Antiquary* (Edinburgh 1980).

David V Clarke: 'Scottish Archaeology in the second half of the 19th century' in A S Bell (ed): *The Scottish Antiquarian Tradition* (Edinburgh 1981), pp 114-2.

David V Clarke: 'Presenting a national perspective of pre-history and early history in the Museum of Scotland' in J A Atkinson, I Banks and J O'Sullivan (eds): *Nationalism and Archaeology* (Glasgow 1996), pp 67-77.

Sir David Fraser (ed): *The Christian Watt Papers* (Aberdeen 1982).

Professor Patrick Geddes: 'The Philosophy of Museums' in *The North East Land and its People* (Aberdeen 1930), pp 17-21.

Sir Nicholas Goodison: *A new era for Museums* (London 1997).

James Grant: *Old and New Edinburgh* (Edinburgh 1882).

National Museums of Scotland: *A New Museum of Scotland* (Edinburgh 1990).

Victoria Newhouse: *Towards a New Museum* (New York 1998).

Sheriff J R Philip: *The Philip Report* (Edinburgh 1951).

James Stark: *A Picture of Edinburgh* (Edinburgh 1806).

R B K Stevenson: 'The Museum, its beginnings and its development' in A S Bell (ed): *The Scottish Antiquarian Tradition* (Edinburgh 1981), pp 31-86 and pp 142-212.

Charles D Waterston: *Collections in Context* (Edinburgh 1997).

Williams Committee: *A Heritage for Scotland* (Edinburgh 1981).

## National Museums of Scotland: reports and documents (chronologically)

Robert Saddler: 'Planetaria' – synopsis of a study tour to the Carl Zeiss Foundation, MOPBW (Edinburgh 1968).

File extracts regarding Museum proposals, 1969-71, The Royal Fine Art Commission for Scotland.

Trevor Mann: 'Royal Scottish Museum future development Feasibility Study' (March 1971).

Trevor Mann: 'Royal Scottish Museum future development Feasibility Study Mark 2' (June 1972).

Royal Scottish Museum: 'Triennial Report' (December 1973).

Trevor Mann: 'Royal Scottish Museum future development Feasibility Study Mark 3' (March 1978).

'Museums Advisory Board Report to the Secretary of State', Scottish Education Dept (Edinburgh 1985).

'The Proposed Museum of Scotland': Report of the New Buildings Working Group (the Cramond Group) (March 1987, NMS [87]7).

'St Andrew: will he ever see the light?' (Edinburgh n.d.).

John Richards 'Feasibility Study. The Museum of Scotland' (August 1989).

'Museum of Scotland Option Appraisal' by Phillips Knox & Arthur (June 1989).

'Museum of Scotland Competition Brief' (1991).

'Exhibition Brief, Museum of Scotland' (1991).

'Conceptual brief – The Museum of Scotland project' (May 1992).

Application to Heritage Lottery Fund (January 1996).

Jenni Calder: *A history of the Royal Scottish Museum* (unpublished manuscript).

'Cultural tourism: the Case of Museums', NMS seminar (12-17 September 1997).

## National Museums of Scotland and others: committee papers

Royal Scottish Museum: Steering Committee file 1.6.0 (1961 ff).

Royal Scottish Museum: Joint Steering Committee files (1965 ff).

Williams Committee Miscellaneous Papers, RSM (1980-4).

Museums Advisory Board Miscellaneous Papers 84.1, NMS (1984-5).

Museums Advisory Board Correspondence files 2.1.9/5.6.6, NMS (1984-5)

New Building Working Group Part 1, (NMS [87]7) (1986-7). Working Group Part II, MoS (1987). Working Group Part 1, MoS (1986-7).

Museum of Scotland Committee and Working Group, Parts 1 & 2, NMS (1988-90).

Development Committee Minutes, MoS (1989-90).

The Museum of Scotland Trustees Committee Parts 1 & 2, NMS (1989-90).

Museum of Scotland Exhibition sub-committee minutes (1990-1).

The MoS Policy Development Committee Minutes, MoS (1990).

The Board of Trustees Client Committee Minutes, NMS (1992-5).

NMS Trustees Minutes (1990-8).

Architectural Institute of Scotland Proceedings 1857-62.

RIAS Competition files, 2.3 Comp a. 1989-91, Royal Incorporation of Architects in Scotland.

Benjamin Tindall Architects box 0009 files 6-8 (1990-91).

## Working papers

Dr Norman Tebble: 'The role of Scottish Museums in Science' (paper to I M Robertson) 1979.
'The medieval church', Scotinform Test Bed Project III: Focus Group Interim and Final Reports 1996.
Exhibition Development 1100-1707.
MOSAICS.
Museum of Scotland Exhibition Guidelines 1996.
Museum of Scotland exhibition brief second stage, December 1991.
Museum of Scotland early exhibition material (box file).
Museum of Scotland Exhibition brief: early material and drafts (box file).
Museum of Scotland Project Reference Manual 1996.
'Museum of Scotland Research Report', Market Research Scotland Ltd 1997.
NMS Corporate Plan 1994-8, 1994.
NMS Accommodation Strategy 1992.
Report Group II Phase I report, Museum of Scotland, February 1995.
Review of Phase I report, Museum of Scotland, March 1995.
'Making a Living' Exhibition development, Museum of Scotland, Phase I report, October 1995.
'Scotland in History', Museum of Scotland, Design principles for cased displays, 1996.
Pre-tender evaluation, Museum of Scotland, December 1994.
Scottish National Gallery of Art & Design: competition brief, 1995.
Prospect newsletters, Museum of Scotland.

## Principal Interviews

Gordon Benson (9.3.1998; 17.4.1998; 2.6.1998; and several telephone conversations).
Mark Jones (12.3.1998; 28.8.1998).
Jenni Calder (10.12.1997; 16.1.1998; 10.4.1998; 15.6.1998; 19.8.1998; 1.9.1998).
Ian Hooper (31.8.1998).
Robert Smith (8.8.1998).
Sir Alistair Grant (25.8.1998).
Sir Philip Dowson (2.6.1998).
Benson + Forsyth Office (2.6.1998).
Dr Allen Simpson (19.12.1998; 30.1.1999; several telephone conversations).
Dr David Clarke (16.1.1998).
Hugh Cheape (7.1.1998).
Dr David Caldwell (16.1.1998).
George Dalgleish (7.1.1998).
Rose Watban and colleagues (4.9.1998).
Dr Sheila Brock (31.8.1998).
Mary Bryden (4.9.1998).
Jim Tate (7.1.98; 5.3.1998).
Griff Boyle (16.1.1998).
James Simpson (26.1.1998).
Susan Mitchell (16.1.1998).
Elspeth Alexander and Flora Johnston (26.1.1998).

## Press coverage

*Architect's Journal* (7.5.1998).
*Building Magazine* (23.5.1997).
*The Independent* (21.5.1998).
Press cuttings file, Museum of Scotland (1990-1).
Press cuttings file, Musée des Refusées (1991).
Press cuttings file, RIAS (1989-91)
*RIBA Journal* (November 1997).
*The Scotsman* (19.1.1998).

# Dramatis personae

## Staff

| | |
|---|---|
| Dr Douglas Allan | – RSM Director 1944-61 |
| Dr Robert Anderson | – NMS Director 1984-92 |
| Willie Anthony | – Head of Estates |
| Griff Boyle | – Design Manager 'Kingdom of the Scots', 'Scotland Transformed' and 'Industry and Empire' |
| Dr Sheila Brock | – Campaign Director |
| Mary Bryden | – Head of Public Affairs |
| Jenni Calder | – Script Co-ordinator |
| Dr David Caldwell | – Curatorial Co-ordinator 'Kingdom of the Scots' |
| Hugh Cheape | – Curatorial Co-ordinator 'Kingdom of the Scots' |
| Dr David Clarke | – Keeper of Archaeology and Head of Museum of Scotland Exhibitions |
| Alison Cromarty | – Exhibitions Officer 'Twentieth Century' |
| John Crompton | – Curator of Industry |
| George Dalgleish | – Curatorial Co-ordinator 'Scotland Transformed' and 'Industry and Empire' |
| Russell Eggleton | – Senior Designer and Technical Design Co-ordinator 'Kingdom of the Scots', 'Scotland Transformed' and 'Industry and Empire' |
| Dr Alexander (Sandy) Fenton | – NMAS Director 1978-84, NMS Research Director 1985-90 |
| Ian Finlay | – RSM Director 1961-71 |
| Catherine Gordon | – Design Co-ordinator 'Beginnings' |
| Dr Elizabeth Goring | – Co-ordinating Officer, Museum of Scotland |
| Ian Hooper | – Project Director |
| Mark Jones | – NMS Director 1992 to present |
| Dorothy Kidd | – Curator: 'Twentieth Century' |
| Dr Andrew Kitchener | – Curator of Natural History |
| Susan Mitchell | – Acting Head of Education |
| Nigel Pittman | – Secretary to NMS Trustees 1984-9 |
| Stephen Richards | – Senior Designer and Technical Design Co-ordinator: 'Scotland Transformed' and 'Industry and Empire' |
| Dr Ian Rolfe | – Former Keeper of Geology |
| Dr Allen Simpson | – Curator of the History of Science |
| James Simpson | – Concept Designer 'Early People' |
| Dr Mike Spearman | – Head of Multimedia |
| Dr Robert Stevenson | – NMAS Director 1946-78 |
| Dr Jim Tate | – Head of Conservation and Analytical Research |
| Dr Michael Taylor | – Curatorial Co-ordinator 'Beginnings' |
| Dr Norman Tebble | – RSM Director 1971-84 |
| Rose Watban | – Curator: 'Twentieth Century' |
| Jim Wood | – Former joint Curatorial Co-ordinator 'Scotland Transformed' and 'Industry and Empire' |

## Trustees, advisers and assessors

| | |
|---|---|
| The Prince of Wales | – President of Patrons 1989-91 |
| Earl of Perth | – Chairman Executive Committee of Patrons 1989-93 |

153

| | |
|---|---|
| Dane Architectural Systems | – Rooflights |
| Skytech Foster | – Windows |
| T H Dornan & Sons | – Render |
| Dane Engineering | – Metalwork, balustrades |
| Swift Horsman | – Doors |
| Hewden Contracts | – External works |
| Thomas Johnstone | – Specialist joinery |
| Haden Young | – Mechanical engineering |
| Balfour Kirkpatrick | – Electrical installations |
| Otis Lifts | – Lifts |
| Plumbing and Heating Services | – Plumbing and heating |
| Johnson Control Systems | – Building management systems |
| Waterman Gore in association with OPM | – Commissioning |
| PDI | – Data cabling |

## Museums of Scotland Exhibition Development

### General

| | |
|---|---|
| Derek Hodgson Associates with Graham Scott and Elizabeth Burney Jones | – Sign system design |
| McMurray Speedsigns | – Information and sign systems |
| AVC | – Audio visual equipment |

### North Wing Entrance

| | |
|---|---|
| Kate Whiteford | – Design of tapestry |
| The Dovecote Tapestry Company | – Weaving of tapestry |
| Richard Kindersley | – Engraving of inscriptions |

### Beginnings

| | |
|---|---|
| TPS Dangerfield | – Exhibition design |
| Kevan Shaw Lighting Designs | – Lighting design |
| The Drawing Room | – Graphic design |
| Profile Glass | – Display cases and lighting |
| Martins; Photobition | – Display construction |
| Derek Frampton Chase Studios Jeremy Hunt Richard Hammond Steve Sallibanks John Sibbick Tim Chalk Ken Skeel Ted Mitchell Gary Hincks | – Dioramas |
| Erco | – Display lighting |
| Roy Manderville (Plowden and Smith) Creetown Granite | – Object mounting |
| BBC Scotland; IBIS (University of Nottingham); AIVAF; University of Glasgow | – Audio visual and multimedia |
| Derek Hodgson Associates | – Design of multimedia units |
| Dicoll | – Manufacture of multimedia units |
| Scottish Natural Heritage Heritage; Royal Society for the Protection of Birds; British Geological Survey; Patricia MacDonald | – Photography |

### Early People

| | |
|---|---|
| Lee Boyd Partnership with NMS Exhibitions Office | – Exhibition design |
| Lighting Design Partnership | – Lighting design |

155

160